SOUTH OF 1

Arts and Politics of the Everyday

Patricia Mellencamp,

Meaghan Morris,

Andrew Ross,

series editors

SOUTH OF THE WEST

Postcolonialism
and the
Narrative Construction
of Australia

Ross Gibson

Indiana University Press
Bloomington and Indianapolis

"Australia" by Bernard O'Dowd
reproduced by permission of Lothian
Publishing Company

The paper used in this publication meets
the minimum requirements of American
National Standard for Information
Sciences—Permanence of Paper for
Printed Library Materials, ANSI Z39.48-1984.
                    ♾™

Manufactured in the United States of
America

Library of Congress Cataloging-in-Publication
Data
Gibson, Ross, date.
    South of the West : postcolonialism and the
  narrative construction of Australia / Ross Gibson.
        p.   cm. — (Arts and politics of the
      everyday) Includes bibliographical references
    (p.   ) and index. ISBN 0-253-32581-1 (cloth). —
    ISBN 0-253-32582-X (paper)
    1. Australia—Civilization.   2. Arts—Australia.
I. Title. II. Series.
    DU107.G54   1992
    994—dc20   91-20394
1 2 3 4 5   96 95 94 93 92

Special

Thanks

to

A.F.

and

M.M.

Contents

Contents

BEARINGS . . . . An Introduction

Australia

Last sea-thing dredged by sailor Time from Space,
Are you a drift Sargasso, where the West
In halcyon calm rebuilds her fatal nest?
Or Delos of a coming Sun-God's race?
Are you for Light, and trimmed, with oil in place,
Or but a Will o' Wisp on marshy quest?
A new demesne for Mammon to infest?
Or lurks millennial Eden 'neath your face?

The cenotaphs of species dead elsewhere
That in your limits leap and swim and fly,
Or trail uncanny harp-strings from your trees,
Mix omens with the auguries that dare
To plant the Cross upon your forehead sky,
A virgin helpmate Ocean at your knees.

This poem from the turn of the century, by Bernard
O'Dowd (1866–1953), has launched innumerable English Literature classes in Australian secondary schools. The arresting
first line stays in the mind for decades between readings. Because of the *élan* of the intial image, one always remembers
the poem as a Western-imperial creed, taking as given the idea
that Australia waited through millennia of destiny until the
English "discovered" it into existence late in the eighteenth
century. In effect, therefore, the opening line is too arresting,
because it stops one's remembrance of the sophisticated skepticism that bubbles through the rest of the first stanza. On re-
reading, one notices that the poem abounds with questions.
And they emphasize the South's status as a conundrum for

the West—the South as both ancient other and younger brother to the family of European/North-American capital. Once past the dazzle of the first line's declamation, the persistent reader might discern O'Dowd's bifurcated Australia, a South which puzzles and provokes rather than welcomes and accommodates the West.

For two hundred years the South Land has been a duplicitous object for the West. On the one hand, Australia is demonstrably a "European" society, with exhaustive documentation available concerning its colonial inception and development. Yet on the other hand, because the society and its habitat have also been understood (for much longer than two hundred years) in the West as fantastic and other-worldly, the image of Australia is oddly doubled. Westerners can recognize themselves there at the same time as they encounter an alluringly exotic and perverse entity, the phantasm called Australia. Westerners can look South and feel "at home," but, because the region has also served as a projective screen for European aspiration and anxiety, Australia also calls into question the assumptions and satisfactions by which any society or individual feels at home.

Once one develops the capacity to see double when looking South, one dismisses the idea that Australia is still definitively a geographical location, to be discovered "down under," "elsewhere." One can look South to find no place in particular. One needs therefore to adjust the notion that Australia is best defined in terms of space. If O'Dowd understood the nation as a sea-thing found, in time, in its natural place, contemporary Australia might best be understood as drifting out of its traditional spatial definitions (South Land, Wide Brown Land, Down Under, Antipodes, etc.) toward an orientation where the nation simultaneously exists and disintegrates in a volatile

key

space-time of transnational media and economic systems. Indeed, it is arguable that, in the world of money, Australia's existence has long been ontologically nebulous—positioned (or "dramatized," perhaps) since the 1840s as a client state to British secondary industries at the same time as it occupied the "high ground" of richness in the primary resources required, until the 1950s, by Manchester, Sheffield, and Bradford. The volatilities of the import/export dynamic have long been foundational to white Australian culture, but it is only in recent decades, with the realignment of trade relations across the Pacific and with the inception of the more velocitous information economies, that Australia's ubiquity—its simultaneous marginality and centrality to the worlds of Western power and belief—has become explicit. Australia is now clearly bifurcated. It is both a long way from the world (as it always has been) *and* it is nowhere in particular, in the swirl of electronic information and entertainment. It is "poised" now as a conundrum for the West—recognizable yet chimerical, present yet exotic: a depot and a clearing house for the world's matter—ideas, raw materials and artifacts—matter which can be understood as feral, as both wild and captive.

Or, to describe the situation with greater abstraction and banality, the world's array of ideas can be understood in Australia as immediately pertinent and grounded at the same time as they can also be scrutinized with the skepticism availed by distance and novelty in relation to perceived centers of power and enunciation. To conscript the vocabulary of two centuries of Western ideology, Australia is presently an unsettled load ballasted with a clutter of cargo—the mythologies of nationalism and colonialism, rural romanticism, hedonist modernism and wildstyle postmodernism.* For a viewer elsewhere in the

*Thanks to Andrew Ross for this configuration of terms.

West, Australia ought to be both strange and familiar, in other words, an enigma.

If the South Land could be said to be the object of enquiry in this book, therefore, it must be understood as an object that calls forth doubt in the enquirer. It prompts in the writer the question: "What do I know about the changeable entity under examination here?" The reading and writing of this book entail composing oneself through encounters with a series of complex and dubious objects, all of which can be integrated *(dubiously)* through the operations of this book to form some redefined idea of Australia—and a redefined idea of Australia also calls into realignment such key concepts as the West, Nature, Culture, Nation, Time, Space, History, Mythology.

So this book makes its way indirectly to become, in the long run, an investigation of the reader's self in relation to a nation, a dream, a time and a place called contemporary Australia, a configuration which can be taken, for the purposes of speculation, as a provocative and fictive model of the contemporary world.

As O'Dowd's poem finally assumes, the sea-thing called "Australia" can be deployed in space-time (as in a poem) to mix omens and auguries in contradictory pitch and yaw. Because of Australia's historically determined *dubiety*, it can be conjured as a model (both habitable and fictive) to think with in a Western existence subtended by undercurrents of doubt and change, neither of which necessarily engenders crisis or corrosion. Return the sea-thing to time and space. See where it drifts.

SOUTH OF THE WEST

1

The Middle Distance . . . or,
The Printed World

In this chapter I want to provide some broad historical explanations for what I see as a recurrent, almost mesmerized, preoccupation with topography on the part of Europeans who have attempted, over several centuries, to define a non-Aboriginal Australian culture.

I emphasize that I am not necessarily celebrating or selling such a tradition. Rather, I am concerned to admit that the land looms large in white Australian culture, and I am looking to learn more about the place where I choose to live. I am looking for this knowledge by examining one of the society's governing obsessions at the same time as I am scrutinizing the constitution of the European mentality that has installed itself in government here.

But how to broach such enormous territory? Let us begin circuitously.

Anyone who has read John Milton's *Paradise Lost* will be aware that the argument and the narrative of the poem take on a pronounced spiral shape. Milton's epic commences in the most rarefied realm of preternatural time and space, then slowly and methodically the plotline twists in onto the material cosmos: down to planet earth, to the hemisphere of European genesis, to the mountain overlooking the Garden of Eden, into the Garden itself, further, to the Bower of Love at the physical and spiritual center of the Garden, to the intimate space of the Original Romantic Couple, until finally, in an extraordinary compression, the poem whirls in past anything quantifiable, into a metaphysical disquisition on the potentially divine territory which is Milton's idea of the human mind.

Now, it is my folly to establish the comparison, but I'd like to describe some Miltonic arcs, both in terms of the way I am about to structure the argument of this essay and in terms of the physical and emotional progress discernible in artists' and writers' attempts to understand the continent they inhabit. The second of these spirals—the thematic one—ought to become apparent as this essay proceeds. But I should explain straightaway how this structural spiral of rumination operates.

The method of argument is common enough. Put simply, I want to begin a long way from my destination, that is to say, a long way from white Australian culture and its landscape. I want to start in sixteenth-century European history, then twist in from there to recent philosophy of time and space via a cursory investigation of the development of mapping, aesthetics, and the modern Western mentality. From here, turning in a narrowing gyre, I will discuss some late eighteenth-century Australian history which finds its geo-graphical location on the coastlines of the mainland. Then, as the screw turns, we will follow subsequent rituals in a mu-tated, antipodean Garden of Eden, until finally we end up in a still center of space and in an unquantifiable region of contemporary Australian mythology.

So, to make a start, let's become sixteenth-century Euro-peans for a moment. For our intents and purposes, a South Land may not exist in actuality. Of course, in other histories and realms of experience—Aboriginal, Asian, or South Pacific lore, for example—it most certainly does exist and it is alive with a rich and resilient civilization. But we are sixteenth-century Europeans for the moment, and Australia is not high in our priorities. What most affects us is a twinned develop-ment in Western culture: the great sea voyages to the "New Worlds," and the first widespread systematization of printed information. Chiefly as a result of these two factors, human consciousness is undergoing a sea change. Attitudes about space and knowledge are changing utterly.

Prior to the Renaissance, the storage and transmission of knowledge in Europe had occurred in a predominantly *oral* culture. Concepts, facts, and opinions were kept available to people through the repetitions of these notions in audible speech. This is to say, knowledge was conveyed in a linear fashion, occupying time. Knowledge persisted only so long as someone was able to speak it to someone else. If the per-son(s) who could transmit those strands of knowledge died or forgot it all, those aspects of culture no longer existed; igno-rance encroached inwards. Of course, in certain societies, a tiny minority of highly skilled technicians were trained as scribes and, in the service of specialist elites, could store information in a crucially different way. But the point is that it was not until the Renaissance that this other method of storing and transmitting thoughts became significant on a social level, in the volatile realm of the popularly "real." The creation of the printing press was to alter the shape of the world. It was crucial to the creation of the modern Western mentality.

This observation is not terribly original. It has been made by people as atlantically different as Marshall McLuhan, Jacques Derrida, and Harold Innis. But I would like to mention another writer whose influence resounds through the history of ideas about communication and imperialism. I refer to Walter Ong, who maintains that:

> In many ways the greatest shift in the way of conceiving knowledge between the ancient and the modern world takes place in the movement from a pole where knowledge is conceived of in terms of discourse and hearing . . . to one where it is conceived of in terms of observation and sight and objects. This shift dominates all others in Western intellectual history.[1]

In Ong's argument, the development of the printing press gives space a new and vital significance. Once the printed word was widely available, knowledge became less ephemeral, less tied to the necessity to repeat it endlessly in order that it might exist. Knowledge could now be set down in space, and it could be *seen* as stored separately from a comprehending human subject. Knowledge could become an object, something "out there," in the environment. Meaningful experience was no longer principally an occurrence in aural time; it also took place within a visual, spatial complex. In Ong's terms, "printing was a technique for giving permanence to sound . . . a technique for fixing the word in space. . . . Space had become pregnant with meaning." Books were objects which, effectively, "contained" knowledge.[2] In simplest terms, the development of the printing press meant that space was now the most significant aspect of secular experience. Space could contain explanations of the world. And, by extension, any space which did not seem to have meanings invested in it was alluring because its first inscribers could imbue it with their own meanings, their own knowledge and beliefs, their own systems of persuasion. It was inevitable, therefore, that the Gutenberg era (the beginnings of industrial printing) was also the great European age of oceanic exploration and cartography.[3] The world was being written into European history.

It might be objected that the conquistadorial attitude to territory has always been in operation: look at the Roman Empire, for example. But on examining the ancient military and economic campaigns, one notes that they were always motivated by the kind of mentality formed in oral cultures. The ancient empires were the results of continual reiterations of power, or "truth" perhaps, enacted again and again over the known world. At no stage was there a programmatic campaign to push back the known horizons of knowledge. Rather just as oral culture was obliged to spend most of its time and energy simply keeping the existent corpus of knowledge in currency, maintaining knowledge inside its conscious subjects, so the ancient *polis* was preoccupied more with the affirmation of power systems within the known world. However, once the new attitude to space as a container of "objective, permanent" knowledge became established during the Renaissance, knowledge became an expansive, accretive commodity. The world became a place to colonize, a place in which men could invest their assertive energies exponentially rather than conservatively. And my main point with regard to Australian mythology and history is that the white Australian attitude to the South Land is unequivocally derived from the Renaissance imperial ethic. From a European point of view, Australia was one of the last sites for speculation, one of the last places yet to be known. It was seen to be one of the last untilled tracts in the field of knowledge.[4]

Before spiralling in on this property, I want to hold back for just a little while longer, to consider how this burgeoning interest in geography (note the word "geography"—earth writing—a thoroughly modern discipline) embodied a fundamental upheaval in the relationship of human beings to their environments. Once space had become something to fill with multifarious systems of knowledge external to the person who was looking at it—that space was always definitively *other* than that person—the space outstripped the subjective limits of its observer/occupier. Unless the occupant of a space were to develop a nonmodern, ritualistic understanding of the location, the territory could be known only by means of an "alienated," rational engagement with space. It had come to pass, therefore, that the modern mentality had a relationship *with* the land, while a nonmodern mentality might be said to be *in* and *of* the land.

Let me elaborate with the example of maps. The modern map is drawn from an all-encompassing, godly perspective. In the scheme of such a visual system, the viewer is located outside the represented territory, placed in a seemingly privileged position, and ready to know all that is available and meaningful in the space under view. (Not surprisingly, this is also a concise enough description of the viewer's relationship to a perspectively composed painting from Renaissance times and later.) But maps have not always been presented in this form. Until the sixteenth century the angle on the land was more like that accorded to a viewer located atop a mountain or hill overlooking the domain. There was a sense that the observer was critically distanced from the land at the same time as he or she was also part of the scene under scrutiny. Such maps show a mentality on the cusp, so to speak, between a nonmodern and a Western intellect.

Indeed, if one looks even earlier in European history, one can see that pre-Renaissance maps, like medieval icon paintings, presume the existence of a reader who is *inside* the scene, not separate and voyeuristic of it all. As B. A. Upsenky has explained, medieval conventions of representation were oriented primarily toward the point of view of an observer imagined to be part of the depicted scene.[5] By examining the layout of icon paintings and relating the figures contained therein to the fables they were meant to illustrate, Upsenky discovered that the pictures could not be made sensible if viewed according to the codes of objective, perspectival spectatorship.

Closer to home, outside of European historiography, Aboriginal paintings from the Papunya Tula exemplify non-Western systems of representation even better. As far as I understand the issues, many of the paintings embody narrative incidents, but they are also maps because, in their depiction of instances from communally reiterated stories, the images epitomize crucial aspects of a complex set of myths which contain, coded through narrative, a welter of vital information concerning landforms, meteorology, botany, and zoology. The paintings are for viewers who can imagine themselves *into* the spaces referred to. They are not containers of knowledge; rather, they are visual mnemonics, catalysts to an internalized body of knowledge, a body which must be known by the viewer if the painting is to mean anything beyond its formal aesthetics. Thus the paintings can be read only from the inside.

They do not represent a space that the viewer can stand outside of: it is not space to be confronted. Rather, it is a space to be remembered, a space in which to orient oneself because you have always been a part of it, and vice versa.

The first point I want to emphasize as we come out of this slightly abstruse digression is that it is not inevitable or natural to regard land as an object or a commodity. It is not natural to see nature as raw material waiting to succumb to the systems of culture. There is, in fact, a long history of mentalities which would probably not even conceptualize a distinction between nature and culture. And there is every reason to believe that landscape art, as defined in modern Western culture, was not imaginable in Europe until the Renaissance and the advent of industrial printing.

The second point is that the nature/culture dialectic is necessarily the one that has shaped the history of land in modern Australia. For white Australia is a product of the Renaissance mentality that is predicated on the notion of an environment *other than* and *external to* the individual ego. This is the mentality that the English Colonial Office sent to the continent.

Once they had arrived in New South Wales, the English were faced not only with an enormous tract of space which seemed to them to be invested with no significance, but they were also confronted with a sense of Australian time which was also threatening and which therefore warranted methodization. It now seems simpleminded and Eurocentric to talk about "the land that time forgot," but two and three centuries ago such an observation must have seemed convincing to a class of people who could see no evidence of civilization or progress in the "discovered" region. The idea of the waiting land served to reinforce the notion that the entire territory

was providentially reserved for English acculturation. There
are many texts to exemplify this sense of colonial *droit de seigneur*. David Collins's description of the debarkation of the First
Fleet at Port Jackson is one of the more elegant instances:

> The spot chosen for this purpose was at the head of the
> cove, near the run of fresh water, which stole silently
> through a very thick wood, the silence of which had then,
> for the first time since the creation, been interrupted by
> the rude sound of the labourer's axe, and the downfall of
> its ancient inhabitants; a stillness and tranquillity which
> from that day were to give place to the voice of labour,
> the confusion of camps and towns and 'the busy hum of
> its new possessors' . . . .
>
> The confusion that ensued will not be wondered at,
> when it is considered that every man stepped from the boat
> literally into a wood. Parties of people were everywhere
> heard and seen variously employed; some in clearing
> ground from different encampments; others in pitching
> tents, or bringing up such stores as were immediately
> wanted; and the spot which had so lately been the abode
> of silence and tranquillity was now changed to that of
> noise, clamour and confusion: but after a time order gradu-
> ally prevailed everywhere. As the woods were opened and
> the ground cleared, the various encampments were ex-
> tended, and all wore the appearance of regularity.[6]

The settlers brought with them an attitude about the
otherness of "empty" space. They arrived on the coastline and
looked inland. Behind them, distantly, was safety and truth,
because behind them was the world that their civilization had
ranged over and written over. In front of them, immediately,
was an enormity with which they felt compelled to relate. And
because Australia is an island, regardless of where on the coastline settlers stood when they pondered the inland, they all

looked toward one ultimate point of convergence—toward the center—the endpoint of the spiral.

The history of the European reconnaissance of Australia can be said to describe a spiral. From the times of Ptolemy through Saint Augustine, fantasies concerning the "Great South Land" were commonplace. As the epic sea voyages of the Renaissance netted the globe for Europe, the quest to discover the Terra Australis was done by trawling away at the unmapped expanses of the Southern Hemisphere. Slowly the empty space was cast over. Eventually, after investigations to the north, south, west, and east, the roughly circular coastline of the Australian continent marked out all that was left to be dredged in the quest for the South Land. From all directions outside the landmass, therefore, the colonial impulsion had been tending inwards, the centripetal impetus being rendered more compulsive by the realization that here, after the revolution of the American colonies, was perhaps the last practicable site for a European Utopia.

Moreover, the myths that rendered the South Land comprehensible to the European mind were ineffably utopian because of a fail-safe device: the theme of antipodean inversion. On the upside-down face of the world, perversity could be perceived to be the rule. We all know the cliches: black swans, rivers running inland, wood that will not float, birds that will not sing or fly. The point is that these tropes provided the alibi every time that actuality in Australia failed to fulfil settlers' wishes, every time that the next encroachment inland did not avail a land of milk and honey. For in the realm of antipodean inversion, hardship could, in fact, guarantee future felicity. Sinners might even become saints. Hence, the convict origins of the European settlement actually validated the peculiar strain of sardonic utopianism that developed here.

10

Accordingly, by the time the coastline had been settled and the inevitable hardships and disappointments of relocation had been endured, the centripetal impetus toward the "reward-land" had not abated. The reasoning ran something like this: If we are suffering here on the coastline, or even if we are merely unfulfilled here, we should keep moving through and away from that tribulation, we should keep moving inland. What is ahead is unknown, but it has already been written into a system of knowledge. Just over the next horizon, we know we can find what we want.

Throughout the last two hundred years in Australia, in effect, Europeans have looked away from the habitat of civilization toward regions that were seen to be uninhabited or uninhabitable. This "national introspection" was always characterized by a keen anxiety. It is not simply an uneasiness associated with the unknown, rather it is an anxiety *required* by the myths of inversion and purgatory. If happiness is to be possible in the antipodes, adversity is to be concomitant.

Moreover, the most mundane aspects of history were working in tandem with the myths of suffering and paradox. Most of the original colonists were bullied over to Australia by the law or by penury; they were not lured on by free will and hope. If a "new world" was to be inaugurated in the South Land, the myths of origin suggested that it would develop through initiation rites which were definitively purgatorial.

At this stage I recruit a contemporary writer to help with the survey. In "A Secret Australia," an essay which is, among other things, an examination of the delicate and resourceful poetry of Ken Taylor, Robert Kenny offers a precise description of Australian geography as dramatic locale for myths of origin and rites of fearful definition.

A place of distances, of distancing, of space felt, not as liberating but isolating. Repressing and oppressing isolation. We spread ourselves out not to enjoy the liberating space but to attempt to fill it and thereby negate it. A place of great longings, populated not by the restless of Europe (e.g. the adventurers of America who glorified in that space) but by those suddenly and forcefully denied their familiarities.[7]

The distinction between Australian space and American space is a canny one. In the frontier movement (east to west, and then beyond) of a speculative North America, the drive to inhabit the continent was a more open-ended, liberative process. Also, often enough in North America, the march of the colonists was rewarded with arable or even fecund land. There was never, in the myths of Frontier America, the Australian sense of a forestalled reward, never a sense that the entire continent was cruelly tantalizing the settlers, simultaneously withholding and offering, drawing speculators inward to an imagined "New Mediterranean," or a verdant central champaign, or a lost civilization. Compare this with the fabled advancements of the American frontier society, where no national myth of inversion and purgatory was required to explain tribulations and adversities encountered by settlers. In fact, from the outset, there has been a convincing cornucopic mythology applied to the Americas.[8] It ought to be emphasized, in passing, how these myths of settlement strategically dramatize colonial heroism, thereby muffling tales of persistent tribulation endured by native societies.

To refocus attention on Australia, by the 1830s the entire coastline of the mainland had been charted and all the saliently fertile hinterland had been inhabited—or at least noted down for imminent survey and exploitation. The inland became the center of attention—official and popular—because it was still empty, unknown, and unexplained, and because it had not yet yielded up its putative riches.

The complexities of the metaphysical and geographical quests that were enacted in the outback can best be read in the published journals of two explorers from the 1830s, namely Thomas Mitchell and Charles Sturt. A man of intense curiosity, possessed of a self-confidence fairly described as arrogance, Mitchell was a student of the classics of European literature, a translator of Camoens's epics of Portuguese imperialism, a commissioned officer in the British military, a practicing maritime engineer, and an indisputably skillful surveyor and cartographer. He was the archetypal post-Renaissance Englishman, most particularly in his attitude toward knowledge and space. He presumed, without question, that the outback tracts were empty pages primed to receive his learning and to succumb to his energetic resolve. It was his habit to "relate" to unsubdued people and places by treating them as objects to his subjective dominion. In Mitchell's scheme of things, the otherness of the new landscape would not outlast the advances of himself and his fellows.

In *The Image of the City in Modern Literature*, Burton Pike describes a traditional literary distinction between, on the one hand, the image of the desert, where culture is presumed to be absent or definitively inadequate, and, on the other hand, "the idealised landscape of the middle distance, the pastoral landscape whose model is the harmony of men and nature, the model for solitude in isolation."[9] Pike's terms of reference can be applied usefully to a couple of key passages from Mitchell's *Three Expeditions into the Interior*. In the first case, as he describes his motivations for setting out to survey the inland, Mitchell refuses to countenance the possibility of being thwarted by desert:

> It seemed that even war and victory, with all their glory, were far less alluring than the pursuit of researches such as these, for the purpose of spreading the light of civilisation over a portion of creation as yet unknown, rich, perhaps, in the luxuriance of uncultivated nature, where science might uncover new and unthought-of discoveries, and intelligent man would find a region teeming with useful vegetation, abounding with rivers, hills and valleys, and waiting only for his enterprising spirit and improving hand to turn to account the native bounty of the soil.[10]

And much later, after months of impatiently skirting wastelands, he arrives at the region which he will call "Australia Felix" and claim as his exclusive discovery:

> We had at length discovered a country ready for the immediate reception of civilised man, and fit to become eventually one of the great nations of the earth. Unencumbered with too much wood, yet possessing enough for all purposes; with an exuberant soil under a temperate climate; bound by the sea-coast and mighty rivers, and watered abundantly by streams from lofty mountains: this highly interesting region lay before me with all its features new and untouched as they fell from the hand of the Creator! Of this Eden it seemed that I was the only Adam; and it was indeed a sort of paradise to me.[11]

The idealized landscape of the middle distance, a landscape that can be understood as an object or a commodity, is in evidence throughout Mitchell's work. The new Eden, which Mitchell claims has been granted to him, is portrayed as his reward for persevering in the topsy-turvy world of the antipodes. Once Mitchell has been requited, this new world rights itself. Having succumbed to the modern European sensibility, the land is destined (in his mind) to become the materialization of his vision of the future. Mitchell does not intend to read the country as if it were a thoroughly edited text that already contains lessons for survival; rather, he sees it as a pristine surface receptive to the stories brought from the established systems of Old World thought and behavior.

The apparent success of Mitchell's inland campaigns was encouraging to settlers, writers, and scientists chasing the central Australian dream. However, Mitchell's pastoral Australia was interpreted by many to be of little consequence in comparison to the promise still unfulfilled in the regions yet to be surveyed. Charles Sturt was the most influential and eloquent of the questers who took no great satisfaction in Mitchell's felicity. The rivalry between these two conquistadors is legendary, and neither was likely to celebrate the achievements of the other. But more pertinently, where Mitchell had stopped in triumph, Sturt had only just begun to dream. In fact, Sturt was to pursue his quest to such an extreme that eventually, unlike Mitchell, he was compelled to redefine and abjure the original vision.

Sturt's obsession with the inland sea led him to survey ever-grimmer desert regions always closer to the geometric center of the continent. Indeed the repeated disappointments that beset him slowly began to seem inevitable, or even innate. Finally he was forced to admit that he would never realize the dream at the end of the spiral. Crucially, however, in proclaiming his sense of resignation, he recorded an insight which refashioned the theme of the forestalled rewardland: "Men of undoubted perseverance and energy had in vain tried to work their way to that shrouded spot. A veil hung over Central Australia that could neither be pierced nor raised. Girt round by deserts, it almost appeared as if Nature had intentionally closed it upon civilised man, that she might have one domain on earth's wide field over which the savage might roam in freedom."[12]

Quite apart from the "revealing" sexual imagery in Sturt's confession, this paragraph gives a clue to the way the landscape was now understood as inscrutable, aridly sublime, the unpossessable desert. The continent was finally being written into white peoples' myths as an enormous emblem of preternatural incomprehensibility, a place to dramatize the limitations of the epistemology that the visitors brought to the place. Here is no easily reified landscape of the middle distance.

An antique tradition had been persuading Europeans to expect something wondrous once the spiralling quest for the southern rewards was finished, and as a result, once there was no remaining physical space to accommodate the marvel in the material world, there were only two options available to the society that had invested so much aspiration in the centripetal legend: (a) either a sustained and spiritually sustaining mythology of the South Land had to be rejected outright; or, (b) a revised version of the myth had to be formulated which would simultaneously adapt and remain faithful to the belief in a plain of exaltation awaiting the utopian colonist.

The second option is operating in Sturt's version of the veiled center. Once it is obvious that the paradise will not be found in the secular world, where it was expected, an alibi is required to explain away the failure. Indeed the failure must be made laudable, not negligible. Almost inevitably, the alibi is a tall-tale, as if he is saying, what you will find out there is beyond classification or representation, beyond knowing, beyond imagining, and you will be sanctified if you test your secular life there and come to know its limitations. This is an early reading from the canon of the "Australian Sublime," a collection of tales about mysteries that defeat yet ennoble the reader: stories about, for instance, Voss's ironic apotheosis, Pine Gap's inscrutability, innumerable lost children haunting the Outback of legend, Azaria Chamberlain's unaccountability, Lassiter's chimeric reef, and Leichhardt's bleaching bones.

These are all legends from the secondary stage of white Australian mythology, the stage when stories of heroic failure were required by postcolonial society to help it make its peace, conditionally, with the continent it could not defeat.

Nowadays there is increasing evidence of a third phase of the national legend in development. The kind of story that runs through the *Mad Max* trilogy, or *The Year My Voice Broke*, for example. To the extent that these films buy into the old myths of outback purgatory, they do so with a witty self-awareness, and more importantly they also treat the landscape not as an obstacle to be subdued, nor as something unapproachably sublime, but as something to be learned from, something respectable rather than awesome. Of course this is not a novel attitude. It is similar to the wisdom informing traditional Aboriginal land-culture. And it is essentially the same advice that Sturt brought back to the cities after he had admitted that a conquistadorial attitude was not practicable in the country.

Even so there is still ample evidence of the persistence of the older environmental attitudes, which find their expressions in continuing attempts to present either a landscape of the middle distance (raw material for a methodical European culture) or an arena for a spiritually sanctifying heroism. For example, television advertisements in support of mineral and oil explorations usually tell both stories: the first stage of profit-making is tough and dangerous, but when the benefits accrue, industry and ecology are shown to integrate tidily and perennially.

The competitive attitude to land probably cannot be sustained for much longer, both from the point of view of sociological and aesthetic plausibility and for ecological reasons. It is gratifying to observe several artists and writers acting on this kind of opinion. (Happily these people are too numerous to mention in a short essay.) In fact, to return to Robert Kenny's "A Secret Australia," to a paragraph where he focuses on the traditions of white Australian landscape in order to extrapolate on Ken Taylor's poetry, one finds a succinct summation of a "new" Australian capability:

> Landscape has dominated writing, music, painting and film in Australia. It has been the mainstream. Even history has been related mainly as landscape. Ken Taylor's poetry is surprisingly not Landscape. Not, at least, a landscape always detached, distanced. A surface of words, paint or sound that in its descriptiveness closes off the land. If anything happens in these works, it is placed upon this surface, the Landscape, and does not happen in the land. . . . . By contrast Ken Taylor's poems happen in the land. They take place there—which can be anywhere—a tin shed, another poem, the sea—but always a particular place. The poems are actively in their places, not descriptions about them.[13]

It is the development of this sense of subjective immersion in place, this ability to place and to think oneself in systems of settlement other than the acquisitive processes of conquistadorial survey, that might be a reason for optimism as the third colonial century commences in the South Land.

2

Letters from Far-off Lands

Two Studies of Writing in Exile

I. "Each Wild Idea as It Presents Itself"

A Commentary on Thomas Watling's *Letters from an Exile at Botany-Bay*

Of all the books that resulted from Europeans' experiences of the first decade of life in white Australia, the most underestimated is almost certainly Thomas Watling's *Letters from an Exile at Botany-Bay to His Aunt in Dumfries*.[1] Issued in Scotland in 1794, *Letters* is an unruly and confused dissertation, commingling mawkish melodrama, autobiography, personal apologia, and anthropology along with aesthetic theory and geographical and biological data (or "natural reflection" as Watling calls it). Watling attempts to speak for himself, but he finds that, in his colonial and convict contexts, this is no easy task. His diction is, truly, all over the place.

Because it appears such a mongrel treatise, *Letters* has traditionally been dismissed as unformed and uninformative. However, depending on the spirit in which one approaches it, the tract can be fascinating *because of* its enunciative fitfulness. The text, which Watling himself assesses as "this heterogeneous and deranged performance," is certainly uneven. But the unevenness is literally telling: it tells us about the pressures that prevailed upon an alien subject attempting to methodize experience at the time of white Australia's inauguration. *Letters* can be read, therefore, as the earliest published attempt by a European to write an Australian aesthetics.

The known details of Watling's life are scant.[2] Parish documents suggest that he was born in Dumfries, Scotland, in September 1762. It appears he was orphaned early and entrusted to the care of his maternal aunt, Marion Kirkpatrick, also resident in Dumfries. Although no conclusive verification has been found for the supposition, it is assumed, on the evidence of Watling's writing and paintings, that the young Thomas received training in neoclassical aspects of drafting and composition. At the time he was "judicially examined" (November 1788 through April 1789) for forging guinea notes from the Bank of Scotland, he was described in official correspondence as "by trade a painter or limner"[3] and as "an ingenious Artist."[4]

Watling professed his innocence of the forgery charges— conviction for which carried a capital punishment. But, in April 1789, when facing final judgment before the Dumfries Circuit Court, he deemed it pragmatic to consent to transportation without trial rather than risk the wrath of the judiciary.

Accordingly, Watling's status in the penal colony of New

South Wales was to be unclear. Although sentenced to four-teen years exile, he was not an officially designated convicted criminal. Even so, his circumstances in Port Jackson were unen-viable. He was treated as an indentured laborer, another type of convict as far as colonial officialdom was concerned. And his labor was specifically related to his skills and his putative crime—he was assigned as a journeyman artist to the officers of the garrison, many of whom were preparing annals for pub-lication in London.

Watling's expressed bitterness at this indignity (he called it "bondage" and "prostitution") is certainly acrid. Indeed, be-fore he had disembarked at Port Jackson—well before he had even shipped out of Plymouth—life had become increasingly sour. Firstly, while en route from Edinburgh to Plymouth aboard the prison barque "The Peggy," Watling and a fellow internee named Paton chose to inform upon, and thereby thwart, an incipient convict mutiny. Paton received an uncon-ditional pardon, but the action brought Watling no recom-pense in the form of the clemency he craved. In fact, behind the scenes and unbeknown to Watling, it had been decided that an artist of acknowledged ingenuity would be a boon to the colony and that the Dumfrieshire lad was not to be let go.[5]

So it was that on arrival in Plymouth, Watling was con-signed to a fetid prison-hulk ("The Dunkirk") in which he was to endure two years before shipping out of England. Fi-nally, when "The Pitt" carried him south of the Equator late in 1791, he seized a few days' liberty by jumping ship at the Cape of Good Hope. Within weeks, however, he was recap-tured by the Dutch constabulary there and was consigned to the brig for eight months while awaiting the next easterly-bound ship that could complete his transportation. Three years after consenting to his own exile, therefore, Watling landed, saturnine and self-obsessed, in New South Wales.

This was October 1792. Colonial records show that, by September 1796, Watling's pleas for mercy to Governor Hunter had borne some fruit, in the form of a pardon which, almost certainly, did *not* include passage home. From here on the story becomes mostly speculation. There are reports of a painting instructor named Watling having set up a modest tutorial business in Calcutta from 1801 to 1803. This venture may have been a contingency measure to finance a traveler stalled halfway on his return from exile. The life story is all conjecture until 1806, when Scottish documents show that Watling was back in his homeland and once again on trial for forgery. This time, however, fortune (or perhaps it was justice—there is no way of judging) was on his side, and the case was summarily dismissed. His involvement with New South Wales was over, as was his time of Australian historical significance.

Letters from an Exile is a document which we can use to understand some of the complicated issues of subjectivity and creativity in a colonial situation. The text (and secondary historical research) may tell us very little that is reliable about the historical entity called Watling, but, in the context of our analyzing the book's utility as an aesthetic document, it ought to be clear that, when I refer to Watling, I am talking not of an historical personage so much as of a character or textual configuration brought into being by the semantic operations of this tract which bears his name and which has survived as an emissary from times past. (Times past, certainly—but times that still exert their influence upon us.) *Letters* is being used quite deliberately here as a tool for speculation. Its myth-opoeic significance, rather than its historical import, is at issue.

The dateline of the first missive in *Letters* establishes that Watling writes to his audience from a far-off land: "Sydney-Cove, Port Jackson, New-South-Wales." He writes from a place where little is certain, where an exile is liable to lose his sense of orientation in the world of ideas as well as in the material realm.

Not only do antique European cliches about the anarchic antipodes appear to be true in this region where Watling perceives the "generality of the birds and the beasts sleeping by day, and singing or catering in the night . . . [to be] . . . such an inversion in nature as is hitherto unknown" [p. 13]. There also seems to have been a dissolution of the cultural standards by which a Briton organizes the pell-mell of daily sensation and experience into a meaningful configuration. Streams and flowers are everywhere "nameless" and "nondescript"; "silence" and "solitude" imbue the world and the text; the word "liberty" tolls dolefully through the paragraphs, sounding a lament for mundanities now lost and undervalued. Within the austral normlessness, the author misses the sense of ordinary things—trees and shrubs one knows, weather patterns that can be predicted, communication with kith and kin, landmarks and features you could find on a map. As Watling declaims, the "air, the sky, the land, are objects entirely different from all that a *Briton* has been accustomed to see before" [p. 13].

If entities as huge and nebulous as the land and the sky are to be understood as *objects*, then the author must be able to assume the role of subject in semantic control of them. In Watling's case, he might have expected two viable options: he could have assumed that the world of objects would fit the schemas that affirm a scientist's classification of a comprehensible world; or, working from the opposite direction, he might have chosen to inflate his artist's sense of creative potency to the extent that no worldly chaos could withstand the synthetic powers of the Muses' favored subject.

A writer in Watling's era might reasonably have expected a choice between these two significative procedures. But once he is in the colony, he is confronted with a dilemma, because neither Science nor Poesy as he knows them seems to be authorized. On the one hand, the objective world that is meant to present itself to the scientist refuses to settle down here into conventional taxonomies. If late eighteenth-century science encouraged its practitioners to regard nature as a book to be read closely and patiently by the educated European,[6] then Port Jackson grammar is a riddle to Watling:

> The vast number of green frogs, reptiles, and large insects, among the grass and on the trees, during the spring, summer, and fall, make an incessant noise and clamour. They cannot fail to surprise the stranger exceedingly, as he will hear their discordant croaking just by, and sometimes all around him, though he is unable to discover whence it proceeds: — nor can he perceive the animals from whence the sounds in the trees issue, they being most effectually hid among the leaves and branches [p. 11].

Or as James Smith, the first president of the Linnaean Society, was declaring more explicitly in the very same year:

> When a botanist first enters on the investigation of so remote a country as New Holland, he finds himself as it were in a new world. He can scarcely meet with any fixed points from whence to draw his analogies; and even those that appear most promising, are frequently in danger of misleading, instead of informing him. The whole tribes of plants, which at first sight seem familiar to his acquaintance, as occupying links in Nature's chain, on which he

is accustomed to depend, prove, on nearer examination, total strangers, with other configurations, other economy, and other qualities, not only the species themselves are new, but most of the genera, and even natural orders.[7]

Empiricist methods, therefore, lead to mystery rather than certainty in Botany Bay.

On the other hand, there is the poetic option, to shape the world to one's own preconceptions. However, although Watling acknowledges that "picturesque" elements do coexist with the "non-descript" features around Port Jackson, he is oppressed by the sense of falsity underlying any attempt to select and combine pictorial elements so as to represent New South Wales as affirmative of British taste.

If Watling must interpret the scene, he would rather be true to himself than to his masters. But his sense of self is jeopardized at least as much as his feelings of fealty to British authority. For example, his opinions on the Aborigines reveal much about his attitudes to himself:

> The people are in general very straight and slim, but extremely ill featured; and in my opinion the women moreso than the men. Irascibility, ferocity, cunning, treachery, revenge, filth, and immodesty, are strikingly their dark characteristics—their virtues are so far from conspicuous, that I have not, as yet, been able to discern them [pp. 11–12].

For our analytical purposes it is not the bigotry in this statement that is noteworthy, but the qualifications—"in my opinion" and "as yet"—that Watling grafts into the diatribe. Even in this passage where he is judging the objects he is describing, his subjectivity is somewhat besieged. He cannot pretend to be unequivocally true or objective in his proclamations. His opinions are relative to his circumstances. As he asserts, "there is no criterion of judging" a phenomenon such as Aboriginal mentality. This is a niggling point for him. Later in the disquisition he reemphasizes the relativity of his judgments when discussing Aboriginal dialects: "To an *European* ear the articulation seems uncommonly wild and barbarous; owing very likely, to those national prejudices every man imbibes, and perhaps cannot entirely divest himself of" [p. 13]. It appears Watling cannot find in himself the overweening attitude necessary for co-opting a colony into an imperial worldview.

In *Letters*, as in some of Watling's paintings and drawings, there is a sense that, if New South Wales is a world of anomalies, then it is the European sensibility which is out of phase. Although it rules by force of military power in Port Jackson, European subjectivity is under duress. Quite simply, the European "I" is not the Aboriginal "I."

Watling craves his own homeland and all that it means by way of referential certainties. But this craving is not simply nostalgia: it is melancholy. The distinction is crucial. *Letters* is constructed as the utterance of a persona who has not been afforded the luxury of pleasant reminiscence. This is not only because his past is steeped in a personal shame, but also because the protagonist is suspended in a temporal limbo which does not allow for pleasant reflection. The predicament for the "I" who writes the letters is too stringent for nostalgia. This "I" is trying to live meaningfully in a perplexing natural environment and in a society with no sensible past that he can discern. Therefore, because he is without the reference points of a history that is popularly acknowledged and debated, he is in a society that also has no definable present. He is in a society that presently cannot be readily interpreted.

As for the future, by definition, it is meant to be undefined. But even this is not shaping up in an orthodox way in *Letters*, because there is nothing like a reasonable guarantee that the society will exist in a year's time. There is no certainty that "future" is a word for the Port Jackson vocabulary. Thus, a disorienting, conditional mood pervades the text. So much that ought to be "in place" for a writer and painter is not where it should be, and Watling is attempting to cope with some kind of semiotic weightlessness.

This explains the urgency and inordinate sentimentality of his memories: "Embracing the opportunity of a returning vessel, I would waft you, from this place, a second testimonial of my insuperable attachment and remembrance" [p. 8]. His greatest (and most reasonable) fear is that he will be exiled from his own past tense and from his loved ones' present tense. The conundrum is that in New South Wales those two tenses have to be understood as identical. Hence the anxiety which, when added to nostalgia, contributes to Watling's melancholy.

It is an anxiety which impels the writer to mark out, early in the text, two extremes of communicable experience. In the first instance, *freedom*, "the jubilee of creation," the "most pleasing delirium that ever was poured upon mortal"; and in the second, *incarceration*, "the tremendous abyss of blackest and deepest of misery." Rhetorically unsubtle as the deployment of such superlatives may seem, it is also appropriate to the concerns of a text which returns again and again to the question of subjective stability—how can "I" make sense, how can "I" maintain a notion of who "I" am? Somewhere between Watling's hyperbolic degrees of felicity and despondency there lies an optimum subjective condition. Watling's persona presents itself to the reader as apprised of both extremes and desirous of neither: "So soon as I have discharged this letter, I shall fabricate schemes for a continuation of humble happiness" [p. 9].

But how to attain such humility, such median subjectivity, in the given circumstances? This question is the key to the drama of *Letters*. Is "drama" the right word? It does describe somehow the fortunes of Watling's text as he employs so many different styles and mentalities, many of them parlously confused, in his continuous attempt to be self-possessed in exile.

There is no denying it: *Letters* is neither smooth nor seamless. Watling writes that he hopes the text will receive the editorial "revival of an abler hand," but the publisher "declines taking any liberty" with the discourse. If the inconsistencies are disconcerting, all the better, for, in effect, the publisher's disclaimer establishes that the "deranged" quality of the writing is integral to its meaning. The readers have a task which must not be abjured: "how [Watling] acquits himself, the public must determine" [p. 8]. The predicament of a writer struggling to make sense in daunting circumstances is thus highlighted as an abiding concern in the text.

Watling's manifest incompetence is highly significant therefore. The text does not invite us to disparage the heterogeneous quality of *Letters*. Rather we are asked to analyze the performance, to determine how the writer acquits himself, and to ascertain what it means for a subject in this situation to essay an argument. It is a dramatic situation: in these circumstances that are defined by subjective extremities—abysses of horror, sorrow, and subjugation that are rendered even more sheer by brief but futile moments of delirious happiness—is the author able to speak sensibly? Moreover, given that his other main outlet of expressive self-determinacy (painting and drawing) has been indentured to a despised authority, his writing is obliged to mean so much more in terms of the authorial persona's subjective autonomy. The pressure on the text is importunate. *Letters* stages a conflict between sanity and impending breakdown. It is a drama that is expressed formally, textually.

When reading the *Letters* in one sitting, a reader can mark out a distinct pattern in the discursive shifts. The equivocation that will govern the entire text is signalled immediately. There are two reasons, claims the publisher, for issuing the text: on the one hand, "it may contribute a little to the relief of an old, infirm, and friendless woman"; and, on the other, the account will further the advancement of world knowledge. From the outset, scholarly discourse is imbued with the hyperbolic sentimentality characteristic of melodrama. Two enunciative modes with radically different interpretive codes are shown to be operating simultaneously in the same tract. One might expect little compatibility between the rectitude of scholarly reification and the emotional "overripeness" of a story about an exiled orphan and his ailing guardian. However, given that melodrama typically represents notions and sentiments that cannot be contained within the strictures of taste and social decorum, it is somehow appropriate to tinge an account of the "indecorous" antipodes with a generically excessive tone.

By degrees, the text becomes stylistically more tangled. The first letter shows Watling commencing in melodramatic mode but moving quickly into a meditation on his subjectivity. But this is also self-analysis pursued for the purposes of aesthetic commentary. How do I feel? What do I know? And how do I make sense of what I see? The questions are interrelated:

In my saddest hours, and God knows there are many of them, I have observed that you are then most busy with my memory. Melancholy's sombre shadow louring over my soul, endears the fleeting moment by impelling me to write to you. Indeed, it is solely owing to this despondent state of mind, that ought I have produced for those last four years proceeds. When this gloom frowns dreadful over the vista of my being, I but too much indulge the dreary prospect—exploring the wide domain of adversity terminated only by the impending darkness; — hence it is, that whatever flows from my pen, or is laboured by my pencil, affects, in some degree, the tone of mind that possess [*sic*] me at the period of its production [p. 8].

The paragraph emphasizes that, in this situation, aesthetic rumination cannot be separated from an analysis of the theorist's own subjectivity. Watling perceives the world to be an outer manifestation of his own sensibility; but, most importantly, he is also aware that the connection is a subjective one and, therefore, cannot logically be called objectively true. Note how the "exploration" of the artist's "domain" (i.e., aesthetics) and the description of his "tone of mind" (i.e., private expression) are not distinctly separated in the writer's argument. Subjectivity here is a painterly composition of vistas, tones, and prospects, while aesthetics is formulated with words like melancholy, gloom, and adversity. If this is aesthetics that Watling is writing, it is of a highly subjective, melodramatic sort, without the theorist's critical distance or objectivity. He writes about art, himself, and the world in order to feel composed.

No sooner is this much established than the text shifts again and becomes factual autobiography, listing the ports and ships that accommodated the writer on his journey to exile. The text's first phase of aesthetics seems to have been completed. But by now we know that, when other discourses are operating in Watling's writing, they are to be regarded as integral to an aesthetic rumination.[8] Accordingly, when the next letter abruptly flashes back seventeen months to cover Watling's brief period of liberty in Cape Town, it clarifies his theoretical and historical propositions even though it seems to be nothing but a private biographical interlude. The flashback may be past tense, but its expression in the present ensures it has a bearing on what is to proceed in the immediate future. If the reader's temporal location is thereby complicated, the confusion is germane—remember Watling's dilemma concerning the past tense that must be maintained as the present when he attempts to preserve his sense of attachment to loved ones in Scotland. In a situation as subjectively destabilizing as Watling's, there is an inevitable debilitation of the will to impose a recognizable pattern on a picture, or on a set of ideas and impressions, that can be put down in writing. Only artists blessed with arrogance or with utterly confident interpretations of the world that they inhabit can expect to shape that world to their own visions when they methodize it through art.

Watling takes pains to acknowledge the unsettled quality of his writing: "not however expecting connection you must just accept of each wild idea as it presents itself" [p. 10]. He has to admit that his self is obscure and changeable at present; he cannot sustain the compulsion to figure the world coherently according to his own inner nature. Consequently, he decides to surrender to the objective world and to attempt through observation and description to discern in it a logic that he might eventually begin to manipulate: "I shall for the time wave [*sic*] egotism, and commence a slight, [*sic*] contour of this novel country" [p. 10].

This is a revealing ploy. He is prepared to act on a belief that would be heresy to a true Romantic soul: he is able to presume that a world might meaningfully exist independently of his own consciousness. Watling's presumption reveals how transitional his consciousness is. Because of a couple of accidents—one concerning his spatial location in New South Wales and the other his chronological location in the "cusp" period between the Enlightenment and Romantic eras—*Letters* can be read as exemplary of the mutation that was occurring in Western subjectivity at this time. With a revolution in Europe, a revolution in the Americas, and volatility in the realm of knowledge and classification (scientific, social, and philosophical), the world had become an interrogative place. Does the world mean because it means, or does it simply mean what we say? Is the world the domain of the encyclopedist or of the bard? Am "I" part of the world and, therefore, analyzable as an object, or am "I" the reason the world exists as object?

Watling surrenders to the objective world, and begins to outline his observational "contour" of Port Jackson and the environs. He commences prosaically, but he cannot sustain the critical distance for more than three paragraphs of statistics and topography. The mention of the namelessness and silence prevalent in New South Wales forces him back to a set of evocative references: he talks again of home, just long enough to be distracted from the "natural reflection," long enough to diverge once more into aesthetic hypothesis:

> The landscape painter may in vain seek here for that beauty which arises from happy-opposed off-scapes. Bold rising hills, or auzure [sic] distances would be a kind of phaenomena. The principal traits of the country are extensive woods, spread over a little-varied plain. I however confess, that were I to select and combine, I might avoid that sameness and find engaging employment [p. 11].

This is only a digression, however. He promptly returns to his empiricist resolve, describing climatic peculiarities. But the descriptions are now illustrated with reference to his personal experience of these phenomena—he is finding that subjectivity cannot be kept out of his objective renditions. As noted earlier, he deduces that he cannot trust the world to *mean* honestly for him. If nature is a book, it is not to be judged by its cover: "The face of the country is deceitful; having every appearance of fertility; and yet productive of no one article in itself fit for the support of mankind" [p. 10].

The circumstances in which a subject interprets a script need to be taken into account if the reading is to be trusted. The consciousness of the reader becomes a component of the meaning of the text, regardless of whether that text is (in our case) a book or (in Watling's case) a world that is meant to have meaning; hence the equivocal voice noted already in the *Letters'* ensuing pages concerning the Aborigines. As his attempts to represent New South Welsh experience have proceeded, Watling has come to value a certain malleability of mentality: "In a word, the easy, liberal mind, will be here filled with astonishment, and find much entertainment from the various novel objects that every where present themselves" [p. 13]. This is no place for intransigent preconception.

And so the deranged performance continues, from a quantitative description of Norfolk island, through speculative opinion about the social character of the colony, down to a personal appeal for clemency and an opportunistic advertisement for Watling's pictorial services, and concluded by a refrain of the melodramatic autobiography that started the book.

From start to finish a kind of alternating current runs through *Letters*, coursing back and forth between the one pole of expressionist subjectivity and the other of scientific objectivity, to and fro between the linguistic figures of the metaphor and the metonym. An examination of the tropes employed in *Letters* reveals that, when Watling is confident about the plausibility of his interpretation of events, he tends to adopt the metaphoric mode. For example, when describing the dejection of recapture, he knows that he can incorporate such an idea readily into his European system of meaning (because the misfortune is not specifically antipodean); he knows therefore that a store of images already exists for him to deploy to evoke his sensations. Hence his references to the "nauseous cup" of misfortune and the "giddy height of fragile human felicity" suspended "over the tremendous abyss" of misery.

Because metaphor is a play of language in which one notion or phenomenon is evoked in terms of another, the prerequisite for the success of the operation is that everyone involved in the communication is sure of the significances and connotations of one of the terms in the figure. For example, if "X" is described as a perfidious prison, the metaphor is effective for me so long as I know something about a prison. I need know nothing of "X" beforehand; I can know it through the metaphor. Speaking in terms of metaphor is, therefore, a process of inserting new or undefined notions or phenomena into a meaningful system. The mechanics of "metaphorization" are such that, with each metaphorical action, the entire system of meaning is altered fractionally, even at the same time as "X" is accorded a meaning. So with Watling's description of convict misfortune as a "nauseous cup": his experience is adequately portrayed and *at the same time* the world of preestablished meaning has been modified because new information (about nausea, cups, and misfortune) has entered the realm of meaning. Metaphor conveys information because it redescribes reality,[9] but it works on the premise that there is a plausible connection between, say, a nauseating draught and misfortune.

But what happens when the "X" to be described cannot find an analogue in the world of established meaning? To take a hypothetical example, what happens when the "X" is something assessed to be peculiarly Australian and the store of meanings is exclusively European? It is at this moment that the creative power of metaphor wastes. This is the kind of crisis that the *Letters* protagonist, afflicted as he is with a myriad plausible doubts about his own synthetic powers, confronts constantly as he attempts to render New South Wales meaningful to his European audience. The beauty of metaphor is that it is an *event*,[10] a kind of ceremony celebrating the instantaneous process of *creating* an intelligible meaning where it did not exist a moment before. Metaphor is at the behest of a speaking subject who knows virtually the totality of the world and is confident therefore that each new "X" can be incorporated into that virtual (or "operable") totality. Making metaphors is a process of naming—one needs to feel a proprietorial right to do it. But what of a writer in Watling's circumstances, cast into a world whose totality is a mystery, cut off almost entirely from the world that contains the system of established meaning, and also undergoing the self-destroying conditions of incarceration? The ceremony of metaphor is barely accessible to him. Naming is the privilege of a confident ruling class (the class that "adhibits" the epithet "convict" to Watling himself); and Watling is unable to accede to such a position even though he believes it is his role as an artist to take such nominal control.

Continually impeded in his quest to "metaphorize," Watling regularly adopts the metonymic—or realist—mode of writing. The procedure of metonymy is not one of redescribing in an event of significant self-assertion; rather it is an act of surrender to the contours of the object. It is a process of *detailing*: this is a part of that; this lies next to that. It is a linguistic configuration in which the described objects "form an ensemble, a physical or metaphysical whole, the existence or idea of one being included in the existence or idea of the other."[11] Of course, on a metaphysical scale, metaphor is somehow metonymic because it conjoins notions or phenomena which secularly do not appear related but which can be shown, via the analogue, to have some metaphysical affinity.

Even so, metaphysics are implicit rather than explicit in *Letters*. Observe, for example, Watling's metonymic ensemble as he scans the environment, starting with a sweep across the sky and then tilting and panning over the plains behind Port Jackson:

> The air, the sky, the land, are objects entirely different from all that a *Briton* has been accustomed to see before. The sky clear and warm; in summer very seldom overcast, or any haze discernible in the azure; the rains, when we have them, falling in torrents, & the clouds immediately dispersing. Thunder, as said, in loud contending peals, happening often daily, and always within every two or three days, at this season of the year. Eruscations and flashes of lightning, constantly succeeding each other in quick and rapid succession. The land an immense forest, extended over a plain country, the maritime parts of which are interspersed with rocks, yet covered with venerable majestic trees, hoary with age, or torn with tempests [p. 13].

Note the breadth of the scan, the attempt to run words out to the edges of his peripheral vision—the writing shows an earthbound author wishing to tell all, but failing to come to a conclusive opinion. The paradox which always bedevils realism is that the metonymic ensemble is necessarily curtailed in the secular world. At some stage, the writer is obliged to call a halt to the rendition. The part must then stand for the whole, and the compulsion to know all about the scene is thwarted. The metonymic ensemble, therefore, is not necessarily any more comprehensive than a complex of metaphors conjoined in a symbolical text. Neither metaphor nor metonym can be perceived as ontologically separable; nor can one approach be deemed more informative than the other.

The authorial dilemma—which writerly mode to favor— is compounded throughout *Letters* by Watling's belief in his vocation as an artist whose role is defined in visionary terms. He would like to be able to produce a text which could reveal rather than obscure a true or ideal New South Wales, but he cannot summon the words: "Never did I find language so imperfect as at present, nor letters to give so little satisfaction; for the former cannot shadow [i.e., perfectly represent or stand in for] my feelings, nor the latter yield me more than pensive melancholy reflection" [p. 16]. If he were not so convinced of his own poetic standing he could more easily stay content with his empirical recording. But he subscribes to a theory of artistic creativity which will not allow him to settle into the metonymic mode. He feels obliged to portray himself as a Romantic artist soaring above the mundane world, attaining the overview and rendering the scene according to his own pellucid vision. It is his job to make the godly connections, to produce the metaphors that reveal the occulted systems of meaning in the world:

> My employment is painting for J. W——, esq. the non-descript productions of the country. . . . The performances are, in consequence, such as may be expected from genius

in bondage, to a very mercenary sordid person. There are, thank God, no fetters for the soul: collected in herself, she scorns ungenerous treatment, or a prostitution of her per-fections; nor will she meanly pluck the laurel from her own brow, to deck that of her unworthy governor. Let it suffice to *Britain*, that my youthful hopes and reputation are lev-elled in the dust, and that my old age will be unhoused and indigent; but never let her presume to barter to inter-ested men, the efforts of the artist, or powers of the mind; for these are placed infinitely above her reach [p. 15].

The ascription of feminine gender to the writer's soul in the above excerpt further complicates the puzzle of Watling's subjectivity. The soul renders the author a complete human being, and bears him aloft far beyond the earthbound concerns of the "sordid" and "mercenary" affairs of the majority of men. However, embroiled as he is in the nascent years of Botany Bay society, the persona of Watling is made all the more unsta-ble by his poetic spirit. His conception of himself is such that he cannot be content with performing metonymic renditions in the mundane realm of Port Jackson: objective reportage is not his role in life. But by the same token, the conditions in which he is forced to work are such that he is unable to "ascend" in the metaphoric mode. His persona thus becomes traumatized; he becomes an effect of his own authorial di-lemma.

This is a subjective drama similar to the representational crisis encountered slightly later by more eminent Romantics, as Patricia Yaeger has explained with reference to the note-books of Samuel Taylor Coleridge. Yaeger cites a passage from Coleridge's 1803 notes, in which the poet is striving to under-stand better the workings of metaphor. Coleridge is writing *en plein air* as he watches the setting moon:

Thursday Morning, 40 minutes past One o'clock—a perfect calm—now & then a breeze shakes the heads of the
two Poplars, [& Disturbs] the murmur of the moonlight
Greta, then in almost direct Line from the moon to me
is all silver—Motion and Wrinkle & Light—& under the
arch of the Bridge a wave ever & anon leaps up in Light
. . . silver mirror/ gleaming of moonlight Reeds beyond—as
the moon sets the water from Silver becomes a rich
yellow.—Sadly do I need to have my Imagination enriched
with appropriate Images for Shapes—/ Read Architecture,
& Icthyology [Notebooks, I, #1616].[12]

Yaeger describes how Coleridge decides he needs to surrender
to some power outside himself so that he can accede to a
worldview that is all-emcompassing enough for him to be unimpeded in his quest to capture the instant of perception. The
problem is that the moment passes faster than words can cohere. Hence the surprising persistence of God in Coleridge's
poetical universe. Yaeger explains:

in re-establishing the act of writing itself within the context
of an order of words and an orderly God who can speak
for the universe and through the human mind, Coleridge
subverts his own pluralising tendencies and reverts to the
idea that the artist must be God's amanuensis, bringing
not only "the whole soul of man into activity," but unifying, symbolically, the whole creation through his language.[13]

Coleridge's anxiety is similar to Watling's inasmuch as
both subjects are struggling to understand the significance of
science and its observational methods. Both poets want to be
able to "read" the world so that it can be "written" more clearly
for the mass of mortals. There is a sense that metonymic description is what a god would employ to depict the true world

but that mere mortals can aspire to such godly vision only through metaphor. A mortal's metaphor might be a god's metonym. The poet's tasks in this situation are, firstly, to discern when he is speaking as a mortal and when he is speaking as a god (or as a god's amanuensis), and, secondly, to decide whether God is even in His heaven any more. Hence the poet's difficulty in knowing when, in fact, he is using metaphor and when he is using metonyms. As Watling puts it, he suspects that he will never "be master of sufficient language." Both Coleridge and Watling were obliged to negotiate an aesthetic crisis that was also inherently theological.

It would be another century before someone could declare outright that God is dead. One suspects from Watling's discourse that he has witnessed the passing, but is not at liberty to tell anyone.

In laying this haunted text to rest one might finally explain the "bereaved" quality of *Letters* in more orthodox terms, as a symptom of the upheaval that was occurring in the history of Western ideas at the end of the eighteenth century. As Bernard Smith has observed (acknowledging an idea from Thomas Kuhn's *The Structure of Scientific Revolutions*), the entire world, Europe included, began to look alien, and *godless*, once the "new worlds" were examined in detail: "The so-called 'nondescript' flora and fauna collected from the Pacific, the nature of its coral formations, and so forth, provided an unbearable number of anomalies for the Creation theory and the Linnaean paradigm. The tension that thus developed between a wealth of anomaly and a poverty of theory is revealed in, among other things, the successive shifts at this time of taxonomic schemata."[14]

This epistemological crisis had clear institutional manifestations. On one side, the Royal Academy insisted that the artist apply an expressive, synthesist sensibility that shapes the world to the contours of taste and established aesthetics. On the other side, the Royal Society advised its members in the field to surrender to the logic of the object, to allow the rules of the universe to emerge through practitioners' diligent recording of the material world.

The character of Watling, as it is represented by the evidence of the *Letters*, is responsive to the major intellectual dialectic of his era—responsive to it, not necessarily in control of it. Thus he is unable to settle on one or the other tactic, neither empirical recording nor interpretive evocation, in his attempt to render New South Wales verbally. His problem, put crudely, is that he cannot be sure what the world means in this place where even a jail is without defined limits. On the evidence before him, Watling could turn confidently to neither himself nor his god for direction in the quest for meaning and subjective composure.

So, how to sum up the "deranged performance"? How has Watling acquitted himself? Here is one version of an answer, the one I prefer. In a new world deficient in recognizable cultural standards, Watling has to negotiate the gradual formulation of himself as a speaking subject who can establish a local set of signifiers through a process of a myriad tiny adjustments to the imported European system of meaning. Initially, very little makes sense for the white community. But slowly, as each new metaphor is tried out and as each metonymic ensemble is presented, the complex of European meanings comes to be altered. Gradually the normlessness gives way to adapted significance, and local phenomena begin to be perceived and comprehended in terms which are somehow specifically (which is not to say, essentially) Australian at the same time as they are still sensible in European terms. The adjustment is a long and subjectively painful process, and *Letters from an Exile* presents a case study of this "habilitation" at its incipient, and therefore most confused, stage. Taken this way, Watling's story could be the first chapter in a long autobiography of a bastard nation.

II. "What Do I Know?"
The "Alien" Subject in the Fugitive Films of Chris Marker

Making a start is always a problem, but it is especially so when one is trying to write about Chris Marker. Indeed, even before I commence here, there is cause to tarry and digress, because, as soon as one notices a *problem* in the context of Marker's philosophy and filmmaking, one is not meant to consider it an impediment. Rather, a problem is enticing, something that promises surprise. A problem is a challenge, offering intrigue and insights. Thus it is appropriate to pause and digress here, even before the argument has had a chance to develop. Such intellectual dalliance is built in to all of Marker's films: it is his method.

It is logical, therefore, that, in the early stages of any film by Marker, one encounters the question of how to orientate oneself in the topic looming ahead. Or more precisely, how does Marker locate *himself* as he brings the viewers along with him? In one way or another, the films always ask: where are we starting from, and how might we make our way without getting lost?

Throughout his career, Marker has concentrated on either the utterly alien or the utterly banal—two extremes of comprehensibility where the coordinates by which you might customarily locate yourself in a pattern of ideas, in a culture, or in a landscape, all seem either so foreign as to be unrecognizable or so familiar as to be completely insignificant. In each case, the viewer has to contend with the initial anxiety that nothing "makes sense" with reference to anything else within the system that you have happened upon. Where do you start? is not just a question of bad faith for someone wanting to write about Marker: it is also an acknowledgment of the themes of the texts.

On the evidence of Marker's film work, you would be well advised to answer the question by referring to yourself and asking where you are right now, both in time and in place, and to consider what you will bring of yourself to the object that lies before you. You start by attempting to understand the contract between yourself and the objective world that you are perceiving. For this reason (now that I try again to make a start), I want to describe briefly what I was doing during the three or four weeks before I started to draft this essay. This indulgence is egotistical, of course, but, as will become apparent soon, it is also in concert somehow with the concerns that recur in all of Marker's films.

In the weeks before drafting this essay before you, I've been immersed in the commentary on *Letters from an Exile*, although at the time I did not know that the Marker material would demand to be allied to Watling. Let me give a new and brief account of Watling's writing. The reiteration does have a purpose—so bear with me, please, as we tarry a little.

In *Letters*, Watling talks obsessively about himself, giving the biographical details of where he has come from, why he is in Botany Bay, and what he has to do there. Literally and deliberately, Watling tells about himself. In one way, perhaps, he is simply trying to guarantee that his narrative is charged with personal emotion and might, therefore, find a popular audience. But there is a more philosophical and theoretical aspect to the self-revelation: he realizes that the intricacies of subjectivity must be scrutinized if he is to make a start on his comprehension of Botany Bay. He cannot begin to make aesthetic sense in this overwhelmingly novel situation until he comes to an understanding of how his own mentality is constituted in the convict colony.

So Watling is concerned to talk about himself. But, as soon as he starts to do that, he is perturbed to find that he cannot make the language cohere; he cannot find the rhetoric that will render everything comprehensible, either firstly to himself or secondly to the readers. He takes pains to admit this perturbation and to find it intriguing. He dwells on the problem of incoherence, and he attempts to understand the "deranged" way his story progresses from biographical detail to geographical empiricism, to biological recording, to high flown Romantic aesthetic, back to biographical detail, and on to village gossip. He implies that all these seemingly incommensurable discourses must be acknowledged as germane to the situation that he is trying to render sensible. This jumble of modes of speech is appropriate to the confusion that he inhabits.

Watling warns that the reader will have to "accept each wild idea as it presents itself." If we ponder the notion of the "wild idea," we see how it contains a couple of meanings. Firstly, it can allude to the unruly, slightly mad, or deranged idea, something mildly threatening or dangerous; and secondly, and simultaneously, it can connote something "savage" or "raw" which has not been acculturated and which has not yet found its location in a preexistent culture. Each interpretation is apposite. Watling confronts the problem of writing in an alien environment: how do you make sense in such a norm-less situation? How do you understand an object (such as Botany Bay) when you are on the edge of it, encountering it for the first time?

The only way to understand such an object, it seems, on the evidence of *Letters*, is to take account of the influences and pressures lowering on your subjectivity: in order to set up an object meaningfully, you must establish some position for yourself as a subject. This is Watling's first lesson about writing in exile.

Apart from the problem of his own subjectivity, the other topic that fascinates Watling is his concern to understand memory and what it can mean in Botany Bay. For example, in *Letters* there is a passage where he sends his greetings to all his loved ones back in Scotland. To paraphrase a rather complex interlude, he says, I'm talking to you now, but you will get the message later, and I want you to regard this as unequivocally in the present tense when you receive it in the future; you'll know it's in the past, but I want you to regard it as present; your past tense is my present tense because of my location here on the opposite side of the world and because I'm living with grief and guilt and I'm trying to maintain the set of ethical references that make sense to me even though those ethics belong to a world that existed before my conviction.

Watling's "problem," therefore, is similar to one of Marker's abiding concerns. In *Sunless*, his film-essay on Africa and Japan, Marker pursues the idea of "impossible memory" during an elaborate digression in which he analyzes the psychologically baroque reincarnations of several generations in the one personality (portrayed by Kim Novak) in the famous "rings of time" sequence from Alfred Hitchcock's *Vertigo*. Similarly in *La Jetée*, Marker's science fiction film from the 1960s, he develops a story out of the "unthinkable" conceit of a man who recalls being present, as a child, at his own death as an adult. Once again it is a problem of orientation: how might we cope if we had to locate ourselves outside of simple, discrete categories of time?

For both Watling and Marker, therefore, the question of subjective orientation is paramount. How do you start when you are obliged to talk about such matters? The first answer is that you look to yourself and you try to make connections between your subjective constitution and the wider world of meaning. You try to get your bearings on the edge of the terrain that you are about to enter.

With this venturesome spirit in mind, I ask you to stay with me while I make a quick edit, which is an appropriate ploy when talking about Marker, given the montagist tactics that have always been the hallmark of his filmmaking. Marker's predilection for the astounding conjunction places him clearly in the French aesthetic tradition encapsulated so neatly by Jean Cocteau's proclamation that all a poet has to do is "astonish us."

So, the edit: three quotes from three different Chris Marker films. Firstly, from *Letter from Siberia* (1958/59), the celebrated opening declaration, "I write to you from a far-off land," a statement that nowadays sounds like the filmmaker accurately plotting his career for the next thirty years. Next, from *Le Joli Mai* (1963): early on in the film the camera scans the architecture of central Paris while the commentary ponders, "Is this the most beautiful city in the world? One would like to see it as if for the first time. For instance, at dawn." Thirdly, in *Sunless* (1983), in one of the Japanese sections, where the cinematographer is out in the parks on a Sunday morning, looking at the *takinoko* children performing their robotic dances to rock 'n' roll music: he focuses on the child who is being inducted into the cult, and the commentary interprets, "A little *takinoko* girl learns for the first time the customs of her planet."

If we can think as if we're at a film for a moment, why have I abutted the Watling text with these three Marker quotes? There are a couple of reasons. Firstly, I want to introduce the question of heterogeneity, so that I can begin to analyze what happens when elements that seem totally dissimilar are yoked together in a discourse that you want to trust even as you are assailed by a series of visual and aural conjunctions which, initially, at least, does not appear to mean anything. And secondly, I want to indicate how both Watling and Marker are best understood as new arrivals on a foreign planet—both dramatize the processes by which we can come to know an other culture and both seek to find meaning in the customs of the planet that they have landed on.

To elaborate on this second reason, I want to locate Marker in the intellectual culture in which he works, the culture in which his project makes most sense. So I'd like to talk about the tradition of phenomenology and how it relates to an Australian's understanding of the ways truth is told in a situation of colonization or exile.

We have to acknowledge straightaway that Marker is a product of French intellectual traditions, and we must attempt to take account of this milieu in which the films have been produced. Most importantly we have to understand the differences that are operating traditionally between an Anglo-Saxon and a French worldview.

In white Australia, our philosophies have been predominantly "commonsense," empiricist ones. We may not believe

47

in them anymore—one of the fascinating aspects of the younger generations of contemporary white Australians is that they are drifting more and more quickly away from the eighteenth-century Englishman's view of the world—and we may now say, either with celebration or with consternation, that we are no longer aligned to any one overriding "master" philosophy. But our understanding of realism (and, by extension, of documentary cinema) in this country has been directed almost exclusively through the British, pragmatist traditions of philosophy, specifically through Johnsonian prejudices about "concrete" actuality. The sense of the solid, rock-hard "given-ness" of the world is unquestioned in most modes of realism in white Australian culture, and especially in documentary filmmaking which has been governmentally supported in Australia for four decades in accordance with guidelines established by John Grierson, one of the most granitic of all the British realists.

It is crucial to keep one's philosophical heritage in mind when meeting Marker coming from the other direction, for Marker comes from the discourse of phenomenology. His background is in a school of thought which presupposes that if you are going to talk about objectivity, you are obliged to take account of your subjective understanding by acknowledging that the only way you can know an objective world is through your own perceptive and synthetic capabilities. So the assumption that dominates the Anglo-Saxon empiricist tradition—about the pre-existence of the real world—is a topic that does not figure crucially in the set of references defining phenomenology. In phenomenological terms, even if a real world does exist independently of the subject perceiving it, there is no point in analyzing it without first taking account of the subjectivity doing the perception. Any investigation of objectivity becomes, almost immediately, an investigation of subjectivity and the conditions of perception.

This leads me further off the straight and narrow for a moment as I note how Marker's intellectual affiliations can be traced back to a particular strain of the phenomenological enterprise, namely the essayist mode of investigation. And as soon as I mention such a "school," I am obliged to talk about an extraordinary father figure. I indicated, in passing, the paternal status of John Grierson in the Anglo-Saxon documentary school. Similarly, anyone interested in French intellectual traditions needs to heed the influence of Michel de Montaigne, who is arguably the progenitor of the modern essayist mode of thought.

Montaigne's famous motto, *"Que scais-je"* ("What do I know?"), which he had inscribed on his family medallion, was an attempt to sum up his belief that the investigation of the world and its meaning is inevitably an investigation of one's own subjectivity and intelligence. One reason that Montaigne is still so illuminating nowadays is that he was historically placed, like Watling, in an era of extreme change in the history of European ideas. He was a sensitive tablet upon which the complexities of a crucial phase of the history of ideas were scored.

Montaigne was writing throughout the late sixteenth century, at a time when the attitudes about subjectivity, which we now understand as the modern European ideas of personality and psychology, were just beginning to develop. It was the epoch of the first industrial printing presses, a time of refinement for systems of perspectival representation, and the era of the great oceanic explorations of the seafaring powers, all of which forced Europeans to begin to understand themselves as not the entire, self-sufficient universe, but as entities on the edge of a huge realm of space and experience—entities who must maintain a relation to an objective world external to themselves. Montaigne happened to be thinking his way through a time of radical intellectual change. The medieval worldview, in which people had a more elemental or animistic notion of self-in-the-world was in eclipse. Montaigne could discern a shift in subjectivity away from medieval notions of a collective or pantheistic personality, toward the modern configuration of a subjectivity which could contemplate itself as a discrete unit in the larger objective world. In linguistic terms, the transformation from the medieval to the modern Western intellect was represented in a shift from the *ce suis-je* of pre-Renaissance parlance to the modern configuration, *c'est moi,* in which the subject asserts itself by being able to affirm its own existence as an object.[15]

Montaigne was writing at a time of uncertainty, a time of doubt and potential change. Whereas we who have inherited the empiricist anxieties of the scientific era might find doubt distressing, Montaigne celebrated it as a harbinger of change and discovery. Every time Montaigne felt dubious, he also felt compelled to essay those doubts until he understood himself in relation to them.

This is why Montaigne is fascinated by his own travel journals in which he details his visit to Italy. In these fugitive writings, he moves though the foreign land, acknowledging the strangeness, and trying to make it sensible even as he scrutinizes himself in confrontation with dubious objects and sensations. Similarly, many of his essays testify to his preoccupation with the modern relationship of subject to object. In his famous essay "On Cannibals," for example, he ponders the values and emotions of a group of Brazilian Indians whom he had observed "on show" amidst the hubbub of a European crowd.

He wonders how the Indians could make sense of the European civilization which was intruding so emphatically into their subjective order. He also muses over the preconceptions and doubts coloring the European subjectivity as the conquistadors attempt to make sense of the New World. The essay thus becomes an elaborate analysis of the subjectivity *and* objectivity of Indians *and* Europeans. It can be regarded as Montaigne's self-education in the customs of his own alien planet, or as his attempt to see his world as if for the first time, or as his dispatch from the far-off land of his own skepticism.

Given Chris Marker's predilection for the exotic, the paradoxical, and the doubtful, it is clear that his lineage must be traced back to Montaigne. It is evident, also, that we can begin to deal with the subject of Chris Marker only now that we have acknowledged the intricacy of the debates around subjectivity and objectivity in the French essayist tradition.

As all the evidence presented so far would lead us to suspect, Marker's biographical details are not simple or straightforward. A typical Anglo-Saxon account of a man's life might begin at day one and trace the fortunes of the singular character through to the culmination. We might expect to treat the man as a particular objective entity. But as soon as we try to present the persona of Marker, we encounter the peculiarities of the tradition that he has inherited. Subjectivity and objectivity are inevitably unstable, blurred, and interrelated in any description of the entity known as "Chris Marker." He is a dubious personality.

Marker's real name is Christian Francois Bouche-Villeneuve. It seems he adopted his *nom de plume* in the early 1950s when he was a member of a loosely constituted collection of artists known as the Left Bank Group, who were concerned to marry an enthusiasm for innovative aesthetics with a commitment to a pragmatic socialism. Group members included Alain Resnais and Armand Gatti.

An occasional member of the Left Bank Group was Marguerite Duras, whose biographical "self-management" throughout her career has functioned similarly to Marker's process of "self-invention." Both "characters" have manipulated their proper names in order to emphasize, to themselves at least, the mutability of their subjectivity. In the case of Duras (whose birth certificate bears the name Marguerite Donnadieu), her *nom de plume* is a problematic sound for orthodox French pronunciation, and it is only through an arbitrary decision that one can decide to render the title as "du race," which immediately calls forth questions of national origin and historical allegiance. Where does this woman come from? the name tends to ask. Similarly Marker chose for himself a French infinitive form of an English verb, a titular configuration which is poised to become active, a word which cannot be clearly categorized as either noun or verb, but which carries undeniable connotations of survey and cultural reference. Moreover, Marker's chameleon qualities extend further. It seems that all through the 1960s, he wrote regular reviews for *Esprit* and *Cahiers du Cinema* under an array of pseudonyms that have never been divulged. Also, before he became involved in filmmaking, he was a novelist and a literary critic, and he has been the editor of the *Petite Planète* series of travel-books for the Editions du Seuil publishing house.

Clearly, it is a peripatetic persona that goes by the name of Marker: the notion of travel is vital to him. His motto might be found in *Letter from Siberia* when he proclaims that "a hiker walking in a straight line is always certain to get lost in the forest." Like Montaigne, Marker is principally interested in the *essaying* course that is facilitated by the pursuit of doubt. It is the quest rather than the quarry which appeals to him most.

In the process of following Marker's excursions, one encounters the problem of the heterogeneity of his ensembles of ideas and images. For example, in *Sunless*, when a shot of children walking along a road in Iceland is linked to some NASA footage of military hardware via a brief interlude of black leader, how is the film's argument proceeding and how is meaning arising while the commentary contends that this visual material has finally found its place in a film about happiness and memory? How does the film evoke an understanding of some of the influences and beliefs that subtend a phenomenon like happiness? How does one investigate happiness once one has decided that it is a material construct and not an ineffable natural occurrence? (One remembers the aside in *Le Joli Mai*, when the voice contends that "for two centuries now, happiness has been a new idea in Europe, and people are still getting used to it.") The answer, of course, is not simple or direct. It lies in an ongoing pattern of questions and speculations concerned with analyzing one's self and one's location in the world of material and ideas. One must put together all the elements that seem to come within the purview of the topic under analysis. So in the case of happiness, we would have to examine the enigma by taking account of sadness, frustration, power, and so on. We must be prepared to try every intuition and clue that turns up. What one has to do, therefore, is use one's *wit*.

I have chosen this word "wit" advisedly, for, at roughly the same time that Montaigne was assaying his doubts in France, the metaphysical poets in England (John Donne, Andrew Marvell, and George Herbert, for example) were also responding to the radical changes sweeping through their world of ideas. The metaphysical poets developed a style of thinking and writing which celebrated the process of creating conceits, or elaborate metaphors, which yoked together ideas or images that seemed initially to be absolutely incongruous. It was a process of forcing meaning to arise through the application of the poet's *wit*. To take an example from one of John Donne's poems, wit is the faculty which would allow a reader to understand something as complicated as love by comparing it to the workings of a mathematical compass. The establishment and assaying of the conceit can provide the structure for an intricate investigation of a complex theme. Wit is the ability to construct astonishing conceits which reveal or redescribe aspects of experience which our mundane sensibilities would not perceive as existent or significant.

When one thinks of Marker's filmwork, the concept of metaphysical wit is useful. It explains what is happening when the editor of *Sunless* can abut images of children and military behemoths in order to learn more about happiness. The witty conjunction of these speciously incongruous images provides us with fresh and startling analogues for the fragile state of felicity. The notion of wit can lead us, therefore, to a more detailed analysis of metaphor, the trope that predominates in Marker's work.

In metaphor, a phenomenon or idea is presented in terms of another phenomenon or idea. As detailed in our reading of Watling's *Letters*, metaphor is customarily defined in contrast to metonymy, which is generally accepted to be the other governing trope of language. Metonymy is the "condensation" by which something is presented in terms of its "environmental" configuration, in terms of what the rendered object is part of and contiguous to. Metonymy tends to predominate in realist discourse, whereas metaphor works to render the real world unfamiliar.

The tradition of poetry ruled by Cocteau's injunction to "astonish us" tends to be predominantly metaphoric. In such a tradition, the poet is obliged to point out meaningful connections between objects where those connections have not been immediately apparent. The poet is obliged to ascribe comprehensible names to all the unfamiliar aspects of the world and he is obliged to render the over-familiar aspects new and wondrous. So, if I say that XXX is a Bengal tiger, if I have metaphorized well, I have given rise to startling new information about both XXX and the Bengal tiger. I will have uncovered a previously occulted connection between these components of the universal ensemble. Through my participation in the "event" of the metaphor, I will have glimpsed the illusion of omniscience in the world of meaning.

So, to come back to the main road of this essay on Marker, the question of how metaphor functions in Marker's filmmaking is another reason why I commenced the investigation by referring to Watling's *Letters*. Not only is Marker a legatee of Montaigne, he is also clearly an heir to the ambivalent cults of exoticism that defined early Romanticism, the contradictions and complications of which were manifested so "traumatically" in Watling's "deranged" writing. Marker's films show that he knows he must metaphorize well in order to present an illuminating overview of the complex social and political issues that he takes as his objects each time he leads his own subjectivity into "foreign territory." He knows that the more connections he can establish—the more metaphors he can enact well—the more comprehensive and comprehensible the world becomes to himself and his audience. This investigative ambition ties him also to the French Romanticism prefigured most flamboyantly by the Marquis de Sade, whose material can be read as a perverse attempt to tell *everything*, to make *all* the connections possible in the world, starting at the anatomical level. Eventually one might have the broadest overview of experience so that one could see the world in metonymic terms as part of the universal ensemble. It is the school of Romanticism that grew logically (as mad as it was) out of the encyclopedic mentality of the French Enlightenment.[16]

But to return to Marker yet again, the only way his associative ambition can be satisfied in his work is through the yoking together of all the speciously heterogeneous images and sounds that arise during his pursuit of an understanding of the relationship between himself and the worlds of, say, happiness and memory as they are assayed and connected in *Sunless*.

In *Letter from Siberia*, Marker referred to "the poetry of ideas." It is a notion that has become axiomatic with him. When he is in the far-off land, the only project that *makes sense* is his continuous attempt to astonish us (and himself) by putting together patterns of metaphors so that he can build up a sensible ensemble of Siberia, himself, and the whole world of lived experiences. Through such persistence, he might come to a clearer understanding of why, in a startling montage early in *Letter from Siberia*, he discovers on the editing bench that it is "right" to cut from a shot of a fox turning its head toward the horizon so that the succeeding shot presents an image of an eagle flying out of the space occupied by the fox an instant earlier. He might come to understand more rationally the intuition which so accurately prompted him, in the midst of his ruminations about the inscrutability of Siberia, to transmute the cunning landbound fox into an all-seeing presence high above the human domain. Or, to take a different example, we might be able to understand more clearly Marker's fascination for classical Japanese poetry, which he lauds because it "never modifies, [because] there is a way of saying boat, rock, mist, crow, hail, heron, chrysanthemum that includes them all." Similarly with an interlude later in *Sunless*, when he ponders the Tokyo commuter train gorged with dozing passengers adrift in remembrance from their television-flooded lives: "the train inhabited by sleeping people puts together all the dreams and makes a single film of them." This could be Marker's definition of his own practice: through persistent metaphoric activity, a significant ensemble builds up so that his films become trains of heterogeneous, yet related, images and sounds.

Each Marker film has to be a configuration of metaphors. No film can be a totally "realistic" or "all-seeing" ensemble. Only a god could comprehend *everything* in the universal, metonymic ensemble. In the secular world, the writer or editor must at some stage call a halt to the renditions of the world. The part must then stand for the whole, and the compulsion to know all about the scene (the compulsion to be godly, in Coleridge's terms) will be thwarted yet again.

Because we are frail and human, our glimpses, through metaphor, of the startling connections that subtend the world of meaning can never be run together in some kind of total cinema to form anything like absolute knowledge. An essay is valid and veritable so long as it does not end. This is how one can interpret Marker's career as an ongoing essay. In the phenomenological tradition, the "real" is worth considering only if one pays attention principally to one's subjective positioning in relation to an objective realm. If the real world exists it is to be analyzed through the self. As long as the self continues to exist, the investigation of the world cannot be said to have finished. This is the poetry of ideas.

So, to begin to conclude this particular phase of my own meditation on the work of Marker, I'd like to bring us back to Watling's *Letters* in order to ponder for one last time what it means to yoke these seemingly heterogeneous subjects—Watling and Marker—together. In terms of the similarities they share, both are unmistakably "writers in exile," sending their letters back from far-off lands—in Watling's case, from Botany Bay and the guilt-stricken past; in Marker's case from Siberia, China, Israel, Cuba, Africa, Japan, and the future.[17] They share a compulsion to subdue the normlessness of exile.

But this similarity also gives a clue to the crucial difference between the two essayists. Marker *chooses* to locate himself in alien territory; he has enough subjective confidence to expect that his philosophical and aesthetic systems will bear up under the initial confusion. Like any poet who metaphorizes well, he knows that his worldview will be modified slightly in the process of rendering the new object comprehensible in terms of existent knowledge: when I say that XXX is a Bengal tiger, XXX is defined comprehensively, and the tiger has also accrued a new veneer of meaning. But Marker is confident that his world will not reel askew and that he will be able to survive the venture elegantly and eloquently. Indeed he invariably does so, with panache. When Marker brings his European sensibility to, say, Siberia, he expects that his consciousness will bear up under the pressure even though his worldview will be changed slightly by the encounter.

Watling, by contrast, has no subjective choice about his exile. He is powerless in Botany Bay. Moreover, as a result of the shame of his conviction, he has been forcibly divested of his "old world" criteria. The place and the time he calls "home" have banished him. Consequently, his writing is fated to be disconcerting and "wild"; his work cannot be comforting to a reader looking to affirm the significance of the European sensibility. Watling's enunciative crudity is at odds with the beauty and decorum that prevail in Marker's masterly essays, where the viewers and hearers can surrender themselves to the crystalline logic and feel content in the knowledge that each film will become a meaningful journey.

But the debit side of Marker's eloquence is the undeniably "imperial" effect of his confidence in the far-off lands: whenever he manages to understand and interpret the "other" or "foreign" objects that he encounters, he has incorporated them in his own established epistemology. Foreignness is dispelled by the visitor's subjectivity as soon as the newcomer attains coherence. When Marker manages to make sense of Siberia as a "topsy-turvy world" where normal decorums are flaunted—where, for example, houses move to their tenants on sleds, and where wild animals are brought into the compounds and fed for a year so that they can be released and hunted down next season—there is the danger that his apprehension of such "abnormality" is occulting other aspects of the experience that may be more in sympathy with a *Siberian* worldview. Eloquence is often won at the expense of "wildness," and coherence in exile might be the result of an arrogant refusal to learn a new language.

This calls up the question of the meaning of coherence, particularly when we are discussing the essayist mode of rendering the objective world through the oblique investigation of one's subjectivity. How composed is the person analyzing the subject and object? How coherent is Watling? How coherent is Marker? With a discourse as assured as Marker's, what does it mean when such speech, which is delivered in and about an alien land, sounds so accomplished? What is lost when so much clarity is achieved?

These questions are niggling and not easily allayed, and for that reason they are to be essayed—and, therefore, they are to be pursued with alacrity if we are to remain faithful to the enlivening, utopian aspects of the essayist project. As an investigation twists and wanders, there is no reason to grow despondent at the discovery of problems inherent to it. Accordingly, given that this particular installment of the Marker essay must now finish, I'd like to conclude on an uplifting note sounded in concert with a quick polemic about cultural politics.

As remarked earlier, Marker's involvement in the Left Bank Group during the 1950s indicated his concern to be ever-mindful of the political efficacy of cultural work. One might expect that such an inclination would lead to a doctrinal, "instructive" style of filmmaking. Characteristically, however, Marker has chosen the more indirect way. He has consistently expounded, espoused, and documented the topic of intelligence or wit. He demonstrates repeatedly that wit can be a liberating, utopian faculty, and that any society that would deem itself progressive and desirous of change, any society with aspirations to better material and spiritual conditions for its participants, is obliged to nurture wit throughout the communities that comprise the society. In such a culture, people would be able to delight, astound, and inform each other through inventive discourse. Hence, in May 1968, when demands for urgent political action were so clamorous, Marker distanced himself from the demands to engage in explicitly contemporary problems; paradoxically, he chose instead to establish SLON (La Société pour le Lancement des Oeuvres Nouvelles—The Society for the Promotion of New Works) for the purposes of investigating historical issues in new and startling forms.

One of the projects completed by SLON was a short film called *The Train Rolls On*, in which the collective brought Alexander Medvedkin (director of the grand film, *Happiness*) to Paris to talk about the agitptop *kinotrain* that traveled through the provinces of the inchoate Soviet Republic during the post-revolutionary era. The film remembers the slogans and ambitions of the period: "Lenin told us to 'know how to dream,' and El Lissitsky drew cloudhouses for a Moscow of the future." It is a film that bears witness to the joys of experiment and change. *The Train Rolls On* can thus be used here to send us back through our memories of Marker's work, right back to the beginning, to *Letter from Siberia*, with its utopian drives already irrepressible, as the voiceover-chant, "You'd see," ushers in a sequence of lyrical "gifts" from the filmmaker to the audience in a condensed ceremony celebrating the wit that is built into cinema when it is used by an essayist prepared to follow the contours of an idea. As the commentator chants, Marker proclaims that he would like to give us everything cinema can say about Siberia. If, for example, he had the time and the money, we'd see Marker's advertisement for reindeers, we'd ascend in a weather balloon, he'd show us a newsreel of the goldmining dredges that look like caterpillars in the coldest region of the world, and he'd show us groves of silver birches looking like owls' tracks in the snow. We'd see every image that he could find of the long white night that lasts half a year. Given world enough and time, he'd never stop showing all the images and all the connections that mean something about Siberia. Given world enough and time, he would aspire to godly omniscience; but given his human frailty, he has to settle for the poetry of ideas.

The purpose of my wandering back through Marker's career here, finally, is to argue the political efficacy not only of direct action but also of wit, aspiration, and perseverance. It is an argument worth mounting in Australia during these times of economic rationalism and quantitative pragmatism: there may presently be little hope in the mechanical model of cultural politics, wherein one engages in culture in order to have a direct effect on the legislative-political sphere. That is not necessarily a desperate circumstance, however, because what is still operative and effective is the atmospheric model, in which wit is kept in the air to enliven people with an analytical skepticism and an inventive syncretism so that they know how to work with the material in the world while they also work to change small aspects of it. As the commentator in *The Train Rolls On* observes, "The biggest mistake that one could make would be to believe that it has come to a halt."

3

The Nature of a Nation

Landscape in Australian Feature Films

But the spirits have to be recognised to become
real. They are not outside us, nor even entirely
within, but flow back and forth between us and the
objects we have made, the landscape we have
shaped and move in. We have dreamed all these
things in our deepest lives and they are ourselves.
It is our self we are making out there. . . .

David Malouf, *An Imaginary Life*

Mad Max once fought to police it. Nowadays, he's out there in it, simply subsisting . . . and changing according to its dictates. Picnickers seep into it, following the same path taken by countless innocents who have gone missing back of beyond. The man from Snowy River spurs his small and weedy beast in a race to master it.

In all these stories, the common denominator is the Australian landscape. It is a leitmotif and a ubiquitous character. Its presence throughout the history of Australian filmmaking is such that the country has come to represent something much more than an environmental setting for local narratives. In so many ways, the majority of Australian features have been about landscape. Think of all the films that have trudged so deliberately into the Never Never: *My Brilliant Career, The Long Weekend, The Chant of Jimmy Blacksmith, Journey among Women, The Plains of Heaven, Gallipoli, Razorback, Rikky and Pete,* and the *Crocodile Dundees.* Think also of the films that have clearly attempted to ring the changes on the landscape tradition: the *Mad Max* movies, *Backlash, The Tale of Ruby Rose,* and *The Year My Voice Broke,* for example. By featuring the land so emphatically in the stories, all these films stake out something more significant than decorative pictorialism. Knowingly or unknowingly, they are all engaging with the dominant mythology of white Australia. They are all partaking of the landscape tradition which, for two hundred years, has been used by white Australians to promote a sense of the significance of European society in "the antipodes."

In this chapter, I'm not primarily concerned to pass judgment on films, to say this one gets it right, or that one gets lost; rather, I want to understand why so many different filmmakers, audiences, and critics in Australia have been under the spell of some spirit of the land. Why this preoccupation with the natural environment? (It's too easy to say, Because it's there.) What can the cinematic rendition of the land tell us about Australian culture in general?

A trek toward some answers could light out from the territory of local art history. A cliche can be a point of departure: non-Aboriginal Australia is a young society, underendowed with myths of "belonging." The country is still sparsely populated and meagerly historicized. Alienation and the fragility of culture have been the refrains during two hundred years of white Australian images and stories. *Every* plot of Australian earth, *every* spike of spinifex has not yet become a sign in the arbitrary system of meaning which is history.

Or rather, until recently, every plot outside city limits has tended to signify just one thing: homelessness. The connotations are variable, depending on the story, the teller, and the listener—homelessness can mean destitution, but it can also mean freedom. But there is no denying the uniformity of the representation: to white sensibility, most of Australia has traditionally been construed as empty space devoid of inhabitants, architecture, agriculture, and artifacts. It has not been incorporated into the European symbolic order, except as a motif of the "extra-cultural," as a sublime structuring void organizing all Australian culture.

Compare Terra Australis with England's "green and pleasant land." Every Old World hectare has been ridden over, written over, and inscribed into an elaborate and all-engrossing national history. Unlike colonial cultures, England does not define itself with legends of arrival or of choice in an environmental setting. Rather, English society perceives itself to be autochthonous—it appears to have grown out of the soil rather than planted itself there. Having no clear social memory of its beginnings, England simply *is*, in contrast to the colonial society, which *becomes*.

Virtually every region of England has been written into the sentence of English history. East Anglia is not just arable land: it is also Constable country, habitable symbol of the pastoral dream. Cornwall connotes Celtic prehistory, where there was a beginning even before history, before the chance of political self-determination. Even the few regions, like Dartmoor, which do signify a certain predominance of nature over culture, can actually be cited to emphasize how historicized the country has become: Dartmoor stands as the tiny exception that proves the rule about Britain's completely "achieved" agriculture;

Hampshire evokes maritime myth and history; the Midlands are about industrialization and transport; and so on in a national semiosis that is limited only littorally.

English people perceive themselves to be inhabiting a culture that covers the countryside. Australians, by contrast, seem to be neither here nor there. Extensive stretches of the continent remain practically unsurveyed, even as considerable expanses (such as Botany Bay, the Back of Bourke, Kelly Country, the Overflow, Van Diemen's Land, Snowy River) bear up under mythic connotations. To analyze the Australian landscape, one has to move constantly back and forth between questions of habitat and terms of hermeneutics, between referent and reference. In some respects, the continent is a symbolic terrain, but, in others, it seems comprehensible only as "extrasystemic," preternaturally unmanageable, or uncultural.

For a tract of country to be regarded as a landscape—that is, as part of an artistic discourse—the people utilizing it need to feel in charge of it. The land has to become an object to their subjective dominion, unless it is meant to signify nothing but indomitability. The geography must have been domesticated (or at least regarded as such); it must have been rendered safe for human manipulation and consumption. Such is the state of the Old World, where millennia of agriculture have wrought the earth to human design and where there is no question that the territory referred to in a landscape image is already a cultural construct.

In white Australia, however, a different attitude has held sway. The idea of the intractability of Australian nature has been an essential part of the national ethos. It is a notion with its genesis in the ancient legends of the "hellish antipodes"; a notion promoted by the First Fleet annalists who detailed the anguish of a harrowed and perverse society struggling to understand and subsist in a seemingly bizarre habitat; a notion certified by the nineteenth-century explorers whose diaries detail horrid deprivations in the central wastelands; a notion perpetuated, to this day, by the myriad legends of the Bush, that mythic region of isolation, moral simplicity, homelessness, and the terrible beauty of "nature learning how to write."[1]

Not exclusively the field of indigenous natural forces, not predominantly the domain of social organization, the barely populated continent has been figured as a paradox—half-tamed, yet essentially untamable; conceding social subsistence, yet never allowing human dominance. Because it has been presented as so tantalizing and so essentially unknowable-yet-lovable, the land has become the structural center of the nation's myths of belonging. The image of the paradoxical region can be used to explain so many of the inconsistencies of a colonial society. If the land can be presented as grand yet "unreasonable," the society which has been grafted on to it can also be accepted as flawed and marvelous. Indeed it can portray itself as marvelous because it has subsisted, with all its flaws, in this grand, yet unreasonable habitat. It is the kind of myth which "naturalizes" a society's shortcomings and works to make them acceptable, indeed admirable.

As Hegel observed in his lectures on aesthetics, the history of any society entails a continuous process of shaping the environment to the community's needs even as the community adapts to the specifications of the environment:

> Man realises himself through *practical* activity, since he has the impulse to express himself, and so again to recognise himself, in things that are at first simply represented to himself as externally existent. He attains this by altering external things and impressing on them the stamp of his own inner nature, so that he rediscovers his own character

in them. Man does this in order that he may profit by his freedom to break down the stubborn indifference of the external world to himself, and may enjoy in the countenance of nature only an outward embodiment of himself.[2]

Hegel's thesis seems especially pertinent to white Australian culture. It highlights the "expressionist" aggression required of a parvenu society supplanting an autochthonous community and grafting other mentalities onto the place. Hegel's thesis enables us to think of the Australian environment as a developing social creation while never denying that the society is also to some contentious extent a "natural" outgrowth of the habitat. In cinematic terms, it means that a movie screen which shows images of a landscape can be regarded both as the realist window on the existing world and as a canvas on which a created world can be presented.

During the 1970s and early 1980s, filmmakers (encouraged in part by the "culturally responsible" funding policies of the Australian Film Commission) were attempting to create a cohesive view of national character through the rendition of Australian landscape as if it were the one thing that all factions of the society held in common. Paradoxically, however, the same films were also, in effect, promoting the view that the land was definitively sublime and suprasocial, that a society cannot make much of an impression on such a habitat. Or to approach it from another direction, non-Aboriginal filmmakers have often attempted to read some innate Australianness in the landscape even as they have aimed to stamp their own inner natures on the external nature of the continent.

Borrowing a notion from the rhetoric of Italian neorealist film, let's acknowledge "that the place where we were born and where we have lived has contributed to making us different from one another."[3] In the case of Australia, which is such a diaspora of a society, the places of migrants' derivations are myriad. Accordingly, within the Australian community, the sense of factions' difference from one another is undeniable. But of course we encounter a paradox here: there is a sense also, within the logic of nationalism, of the adoptive society's unification. The colony is a diverse collection of ethnic and interest groups, but it is also unified by its shared "rebirth" in the "new" environment.

The landscape cinema has asserted both Australia's difference from the rest of the world and also the nation's singularity of constitution within its own boundaries. That is to say there has been an attempt to portray "us" as one people growing to maturity and confidence "together." Films such as *Sunday Too Far Away, Picnic at Hanging Rock, The Man From Snowy River,* or *We of the Never Never* have said, Here is the key to our identity. . . . Here are the myths that we need. They have been presented as generically Australian.

Such stories (and images) work to rationalize dialectical oppositions: drought and flood, flood and fire, dearth and plenty, enormity and minimalism, attrition and creation, diversity and uniformity, "savagery" and "morality," and, of course, nature and culture (which probably sums up all the foregoing). In such national myths, the landscape becomes the projective screen for a persistent national neurosis deriving from the fear and fascination of the preternatural continent. Because Australian stories have typically presented the land in frontier terms as an awesome opponent—rather than in pastoral terms as a nurturing mother or a placid locale for the arbitrary organization of social life—and since culture has not yet managed to subdue nature (or at least to convince people that it has), Aus-

69

tralian art has tended, until quite recently, to be "anachronisti-cally" concerned with "primitive" themes. Generally speaking, most of the influential Australian art in the twentieth century has barely been classifiable in terms of modernism (let alone postmodernism), where culture self-referentially creates itself from the raw material of extant culture rather than from nature.

Australian art has always been judged to be traditionally concerned with the primary process of turning nature into cul-ture. Of course, resistant schools of artists and writers in Aus-tralia have been affiliated to internationalist modernism and postmodernism—indeed in the second half of the 1980s the internationalist push in the visual arts seems to be becoming irresistible—but, throughout the last fifteen years of govern-ment support of the feature film industry, the dictates of ge-neric "Australianism" have been preeminent.

John Hinde, in his evocative study *Other People's Pic-tures*,[4] contends that national cinemas arise at times of social crisis or turbulence, when there exists a "seminal audience" which is in need of either self-definition or self-congratulation. It could be argued that Australia in the 1970s, emerging as it was from more than two decades of conservative rule and economic stagnation, constituted such a seminal audience and that the unifying myths of nationalism were required and wel-comed by a local population. This could clarify why the land-scape cinema flourished so spectacularly until the early 1980s. It could also explain how the tables appeared to turn over the last five years, when local audiences have seemed less concerned with national definition and when a series of spectacular fail-ures (*Burke and Wills, The Light Horsemen,* and *Razorback,* for example) have eroded the dependability of the genre. One of the paradoxes concerning the success of the landscape cinema of the 1970s was that it gave Australians a stronger sense of their significance in the international arena, thereby lessening the need for reassuring images and definitions of Australianness, and thereby, in turn, dispersing the seminal audience which seems to have been so appreciative of the landscape cinema in the first place! In its very success, the landscape cinema prefigured its demise, or at least its reconstitution.

However, until "The Change" seemed to dawn on some filmmakers and arts administrators in the early 1980s, the landscape myth was assumed to be as fertile as ever it had been over the past two hundred years. Australia could still be regarded as "third world" at the same time as it was "postindustrial." This is to say, the nation seemed to maintain its straightforward approach to culture: that art was the process of turning raw nature into culture. Sergei Eisenstein once wrote with regard to early modernist Europe: "At the intersection of Nature and Industry stands *Art*."[5] Of the Old World in the 1980s, it might be said: Art is the industry of constructing new artifacts out of old signs that have already blotted out Nature. There is no denying that Australia does seem different in such terms. Given that The Change has not yet been widely acknowledged in most Australian advertising, television, top forty music, and sport, one could adapt Eisenstein's adage thus: After repeated collisions involving Nature and Industry, Art is scattered across the landscape, marking, but never covering, the continent. The feeling is still quite strong that the land at our backs is primitive and is, therefore, a storehouse of some inexhaustible and ineffable Australianness. With The Change on the way, but not yet overhead, it seems the Australian landscape is shimmering in the collective consciousness like a mirage, phasing in and out of focus, as a sign at one moment and as pristine nature the next.

Whereas an autochthonous society tends to celebrate creationist myths that thank god for the nation's inauguration, the colonial society has access to more secular myths about arrival and the struggle to establish communities. These myths get called "history." One might presume that because the arbitrary or even accidental beginnings of colonies are so well recorded, "satellite" societies such as Australia would be less prone to the kind of essentialism which argues that a nation has been historically predestined to develop particular characteristics. However, paradoxically, while white Australia was slowly developing the autonomy to define itself as a nonreplica of the mother country, the colony strove to celebrate its peculiarly Australian qualities. And of course, the most enduring aspect of Australian experience loomed almost limitless around the fledgling colony: the landscape would, therefore, define the nation. In trying to differentiate itself from the Old World, Australian society began to define itself with essentialist myths of land. The specific qualities of the nation would grow from the land. The colony would gradually "belong," it would eventually be "in place," and it would cease to be a colony. So the story went.

Because it still seems that human beings have not cluttered the ground with their artifacts and connotations, the southern continent continues to spread out, in many minds, like the text of some divine and immanent (as opposed to social and arbitrary) system of native, *Australian* meaning. If you want the real Australia, look at the earth, not at the people or what they have produced—the erroneous implication here is that the landscape has not already been produced by social actions. The landscape seems to extend unsullied, as the handiwork solely of nature, inscribed and subscribed with innate messages. Quintessential Australia has not yet been papered over by an alien Anglo-Saxon culture. So the story goes.

All this reverence (obscuring the unspecified fear) of the landscape is clearly the result of an alienated society's experience around the ridges of a vast, unpopulated, and speciously indomitable country. But what of the effects? The legends of the awesome land imply that the society cannot be seen to be directing the environment in its own interests (despite multinationals' advertisements celebrating their "quiet achievements" in purportedly taming and rehabilitating the ecosystem at the same time as they reap profits from it).

The generically Australian story argues that society has no hope of stretching out to cover the unsubdued continent. Implicitly, if it is taken as given that the society *en masse* cannot make a mark on the land, then the next most comforting myth would have to be a story of heroic individualism, adaptability, and ingenuity in the unwelcoming arena of national definition—the nation then becomes a motley gang of knockabout types, unified in the fact of their survival but not uniform or conformist according to rigid social schemes: a paradoxical nation, but a nation nonetheless. So the story goes, as in *Mad Max, Crocodile Dundee, Rikky and Pete,* and indeed, in *Whatever Happened to Green Valley?*, Peter Weir's sophisticated investigation of the Australian documentary and pastoral traditions transplanted and hybridized in suburbia. The laconic, "minimalist" hero hews a path for himself, communing with the spirit of the land, reading its messages, jotting down hints for survival, and hoping for nothing more of society than the modicum of organizational support in his contestation with the emptiness. In the inhuman landscape, humanism prevails. The heroes' persistence in the legendary setting persuades us that the land is habitable, but only by a very special breed of people; in mythic terms, therefore, the nation is feasible, but only as a collection of extraordinary individuals.

Paradoxically, as Australian feature films of the last fifteen years have configured this country of the mind, the majority of them have done so in realist terms rather than with a "fantastic" sense of the mythic storytelling involved in the presentation of generic locationism. They have been more concerned with the dictates of the past than with the yet-to-be-created characteristics of the future, or even with the volatile flux of the present. Such complacency of imagination should come as no surprise, given the two dominant modes of filmmaking that have always prevailed in Australia: in the mainstream of feature film there has been the lower-budget end of the Hollywood storytelling tradition—the "classic realist text," if you like—and for six decades also, there has been a consistent flow of government-sponsored documentaries, which (for forty years at least) have been made in a house style shaped by the precepts of a functional, documentary realism. All the other traditions of world cinema (for example, European avant-garde experimentation and quality narrative, surrealism, and the more magical genres of industrial cinema, such as the musical and the science fiction fantasy) have played only minor roles in the history of cinema in Australia.

Realism has been the orthodoxy, therefore. The paradox is that the *mythic* argument of so many of the landscape films cannot logically be conducted through the techniques of realist representation. Take examples as wide-ranging as *Sunday Too Far Away, Gallipoli, Crocodile Dundee, Picnic at Hanging Rock,* and even *Rikky and Pete* with its deliberate emphasis on the interest (distressingly in excess of the narrative at most times) that we are meant to invest in the settings the protagonists trundle through.

The existence of the land in the image works to authenticate the actions of the figures in the landscape. The setting is definitive Australia; therefore the actions and emotions elicited by such a setting must also be definitive. So the story goes: it would *appear* to be common sense.

Perhaps it *is* true that there is a vast and undeniable beauty "backgrounding" life in Australia. Perhaps it is a beauty that cannot really be comprehended and communicated within human systems. However, as soon as such geography is represented and dramatized within images, sounds, and stories, it is no longer land. Rather, it is landscape; it has been translated and utilized as an element of myth, as a sign of supra-social Australianness. There is no such thing as a pristine landscape. There may be an *image* of pristinity (or of beauty, or of innocence, etc.), but such a thing cannot *mean* anything outside of cultural systems. The landscape image might *signify* nature, but that is not to say it *is* nature. The very notion of nature is a cultural construct.

All these arguments about whether films can or cannot present natural truth or authenticity depend on the myth of veracity and trustworthiness that still clings to the institution of photography. The commonsense view that a photograph is an objective *analogon* of "the real" also adheres to film appreciation, especially for a national audience which has been served very diligently by a documentary industry funded and distributed by government agencies.

This commonsense view of the trustworthiness of photography is problematic at best. For one thing, photography, like the notion of nature itself, is a cultural entity which is comprehensible and meaningful because it has long been ascribed uses within social systems such as journalism, law, art, and science, all of which are arbitrary configurations of persuasion and argumentation. Secondly, and more specifically, in the case of cinematography, given the seriality of the motion picture, every image is located not just within culture generally but also within a specific diegetic flow which necessarily gives rise to some sort of meaning (even if the narrative ends up only being "about" incoherence). The photographic (or cinematographic) image is not the unmediated "re-presentation" of a portion of reality; it is a *presentation*, a newly created or arranged portion of the reality of the cultural world.

But still, the delusive common sense can prevail, particularly when a moving picture of a static, seemingly unartificed landscape is presented. It is tempting to regard the image as innocently witnessing all the facts about the setting, untouched, panoramically extensive, and verified over a period of time—simply photographed and objectively true. (It is worth recalling, here, the oft-repeated observation that the French word for the lens is *l'objectif.*) But to believe in the transparency of the cinematographic landscape would be to ignore the significance of so many aesthetic variables. What was the time of day? Was the camera pointed toward the sun or away from it? Were human beings included in the scene? What were they doing? What lens was used? Was there any camera movement? What was the duration of the shot? What was happening on the soundtrack? How did the landscape sequence fit into the overall pattern of the narrative so far? The list could go on. Each of these factors has meaning.

Evidently, the fact that the land cannot "act" on cue does not render its filmic representation any less prone to manipulation. The presented image of a landscape is necessarily a sign. And in the Australian setting it has customarily been construed as a sign of nature (that is, as a sign that is thought not to be a sign) rather than as a sign of a sign. It is this strange negative capability that is currently undergoing a change in Australian cinema. If people begin to imagine their environment differently (not just as *land*), the national mythology will necessarily alter, and that means that people will start to think differently. Then, if you lived in this country, you'd have to ask this question: what would you like to be thinking?

From the early 1980s on, most films that relied successfully (critically and financially) on the impact of the pictorial qualities of the landscape posed such a question, implicitly if not explicitly. They did so with a sense of self-deprecation and with a conscious intent to revise the old myths. Take *Mad Max, The Road Warrior, MAD MAX: Beyond Thunderdome,* and *Crocodile Dundee* as examples. On the evidence of the massively favorable responses to these films, it seems audiences were no longer prepared to take the landscape myth entirely seriously. The films still required the environment to be the principal motif of the story, but gone was the earnest nationalistic investment in the land as the template of a national identity.

In *Crocodile Dundee*, the landscape looks and sounds like the *idea* of land; it looks like a sign. Dundee's environment is a compliant one, respectful of American nostalgia for the myth of the frontier; the outback and its laudable inhabitants are fashioned to this fable of recurrent American colonizations. The national environment represented in the film is thus fitted to a transnational economy. *Crocodile Dundee* becomes a lesson about being respectful of power, a cheerful parable about succeeding through *getting Americans to like us*.[6] If this ambition calls for a refiguring of the generic Australian landscape, the reconstitution of the myth could be achieved quickly enough, from the producers' point of view, because everyone (except maybe a large portion of the American audience) knows that the film is dealing with a sign and not a "fact."

Similarly, but differently, the comic book aesthetic celebrated throughout the *Mad Max* trilogy works to pull the images of the environment out of the realist traditions of Australian cinema. It locates the land in a different system, a more *explicitly* fantastic, mythopoeic discourse. In any one part of the trilogy, the film and the audience both know that signs are manipulable and refutable. Most crucially, signs are not natural, no matter if they are signs of nature. Indeed the *Mad Max* movies can be interpreted as a spectacularly irreverent and effective meditation on the possibilities of change in Australian society, generally, and in the landscape tradition more particularly. The stories take into account the undeniably complex interrelationships now existing in Australia between an orthodox, officially sanctioned "National Culture" and the constantly mutating complex of images and ideas that comprise the international popular culture that gets imported and consumed here with such enthusiasm. This is not to say that all popular culture in Australia has abandoned the more simple nationalist criteria. Cinema and television such as Kennedy-Miller's is still more "vanguard" than "mainstream" in thematic and formal terms. But the popularity of Kennedy-Miller indicates that attitudes are beginning to alter, albeit slowly, across the breadth of the society that gets called "Australia."

A somewhat more obscure film that also bears witness to The Change is Roger Scholes's *The Tale of Ruby Rose*, a parable which invests great significance in the influence of landscape on personality, but which also refuses to offer a myth for an entire nation. On the contrary, *Ruby Rose* presents characters that can only be understood and appreciated as *marginal*, just as their defining environment must be viewed as emphatically *not* generic-Australian. Here is an Australian landscape story that can be comprehended as such only if the definitions of the landscape tradition are radically refigured. In this cinematic "Australia," generically un-Australian types are taking shape in a generically un-Australian habitat. They are there. Either you deny them their classification as "Australian," or you refigure the epithet "Australian."

It is arguable that *Ruby Rose* is the first "peasant film" produced in this country. It refuses to commandeer Aboriginal dreaming to certify an indigenous sense of "belonging," but it still presents a curiously "native" kind of worldview, principally through Ruby's idiosyncratic and elaborate mythology which enables her to understand and survive her "life on the land." The film presents a curiously half-convincing "native" mentality. It is not *completely* convincing, I think, because the style of the film sometimes connotes "European art-movie" in its attempts not to connote generically "Australian" cinema. For example, the "epic" helicopter establishing-shots tend to signify human alienation in an unforgiving backdrop. In such sequences the film seems to succumb to the pictorialism that *reifies* rather than *animates* a landscape. But in the majority of scenes involving daily life in the high country, *Ruby Rose* presumes the possibility of a knowledge of environment, personality, community, and a spiritual world, all of which are inseparable one from the other. The film is not "Aboriginal" (it is careful not to be so opportunist and simplistic), but it *is* somehow "peasant." To be precise, the film does not present life *on* the land; it attempts to portray a non-Aboriginal life *of* and *in* the land.

Bill Bennett's *Backlash* is an intriguing film to consider with regard to this idea of the possibilities of non-Aboriginal acknowledgment. The picaresque narrative and the improvisational performances of *Backlash* set it up as an exploration. The story of white law enforcers' journey to a more "indigenous" knowledge of justice, oppression, and payback, should constitute a radical interrogation of some of the myths that have guided white society for two hundred years. Indeed, it does this to some extent, by virtue of its skepticism about the righteousness of a white Australian judiciary presiding in cases of Aboriginal "transgression." But as the white characters act out their alienation in the moral and geographical environment which the story leads them into, the narrative also falls problematically into several classic nationalist orthodoxies that have always run through the landscape tradition. For example, the Aboriginal woman becomes equated with spirit of place, when she seems "instinctively" to know where the waterhole of salvation will be found in this tract of country that she can never have learned. The improvisatory trek into the landscape tradition succumbs in part to the idealism that has haunted Australian nationalism, as if there is a body of preexistent *Australian* knowledge buried just a few feet down.

Ultimately, *Backlash* seems to sanction myths about the "inevitable alienation" of white Australian society. But it is only fair to say that, in the context of the film's release in the "Bicentennial era," this particular "failing" is negligible in comparison to its dramatization of the morally complex legacy of retribution that will track white Australia until (and for a long while after) it negotiates a dignified settlement with the incumbents who were dispossessed during the invasion.

Non-Aboriginal society now appears to be in the process of rearranging the myths it requires for its self-definition. It is a breeze of change that has been refreshing factions of Australian film-culture for decades. Consider, for example, *The Back of Beyond* (1953), John Heyer's mythopoeic celebration of the storytelling and adaptability of the Birdsville Track society, a community which is simultaneously both singularly Australian *and* as undefinable as the diaspora of all the races and cultures that have made a go of it along the Track.

Nowadays, as more products of Australian culture are redefining many of the national orthodoxies, there seems to be a need for a definition of "Australia" which welcomes a sense of international "contamination" in its constitution. The audience for Australian cinema no longer seems to be "seminal." It is now perhaps more interested in the world rather than in boundaries that could theoretically separate the nation from the remainder of the international community. As the economic and cultural constitution of the society is currently "internationalizing" so radically, the requirements of the national myths are also altering. If you wanted to keep living in this country, therefore, you'd keep coming back to this question: what would you like to be thinking?

4

Geography and Gender

I. Forecast

Consider a prologue for a life-story. An infant begins to comprehend its reflection in a mirror; it discerns something animated outside of the delimitations of its own bodily dimensions. Indeed, the discernment of the reflection facilitates the realization that the body is only *part* of rather than *all* of the world. So, through the agency of the looking glass (and through rhythmic games of temporal/spatial orderliness—say, with a ball of wool) and through the mimicry games that adults seem to need to play in front of infants, a subject begins to be constituted. But inherent to this seeming stabilization is a disintegrative factor: the subject is always to be alienated because s/he is now split from the rest of the sensual, social, and natural environment. From now on, desire will be, in part, a memory: even though the days of polymorphous perversity are gone, the subject will habitually yearn for reincorporation in an all-engrossing, elemental world. Now the universe is outside, and 'I' must find a place in it, whereas 'I' once *was* it even though, as an unassimilated infant, 'I' did not formally exist to know it.

To live, perhaps, is to strive to speak, write, paint, photograph, film, gesticulate, build, or explore. This is to say that one needs to engage an other in order to organize a life for oneself. Implicitly, therefore, human vitality can be seen to be contingent on many kinds of dialogues. A person's life might be intelligible as "human" only so long as at least one other is involved in a relationship (subject to object) with the subject. At its most minimal, human life might be said to have occurred only when that life can be rendered as a story, only when it involves someone (or some thing anthropomorphized?) else at least in the role of an audience, if not as an interlocutor.

This engagement of an other humanizes an existence, but it also traumatizes it to some extent. For, in this model of life, a meaningful human existence must be considered as a kind of writing, and it is plausible that "writing cannot be thought outside the horizon of intersubjective violence."[1] Human subjects are definitively obliged to *interfere* with other subjects, to render them as objects of one's communication. Your objective existence enables me to define my self; but your subjective existence compels me continually to be subjected to an other's definition of me for your own purposes. (And if there are several people in your society, the conundrum of interactions expands exponentially. Somewhere in the social tussle, a sense of composure and collective ease might be possible occasionally, but it will never be simple.)

Assuming we are still obliged to talk of ourselves as Western and familial beings, we must observe that after subjective *constitution* comes subjective *institution*. Social regulations, which are enacted principally through family hierarchies, harness the drives of the emergent subject. The child's libidinous energy, which was indiscriminate in its infantile output, is channeled into the patterns of particular, role-defined desires. The emergent subject, who defines itself even as it seeks to dissolve itself in social interaction, slowly becomes "fine-tuned" as it is located (through chance as much as through design) in the dramas of sexual differentiation most often explained in terms of the story of Oedipus.

According to the great twentieth-century retelling of this myth (in the annals of psychoanalysis, particularly in the versions by Sigmund Freud and Jacques Lacan, portions of which have been glossed in the paragraphs above), the social machinery is fueled by an alternating current, called *desire*, which is a process that is socially formulated, rather than natural, and which oscillates between the poles of femininity and masculinity. Or rather, the current of desire flows *through* men and women, *around* a talisman which Lacan has called the phallus, which in the manner of all talismans stands for many things, including the illusion of authority. As this story of subjectivity proceeds, the masculine exists by aspiring to *possess* the phallus by incorporating the feminine, which is accorded no other role than to *be* the phallus. Each party, be it "masculine" or "feminine" (not necessarily synonymous with "male" or "female") aspires to incorporate an other. It is a question of politics, the differences between these types of aspirations. This impulse

of desire becomes an active current in the social machinery
because the "triumphs" of possession must be reproven inces-
santly: the desired commodity eludes the subject's grasp as
commodity as soon as it becomes incorporated and is no
longer other. Desire is thus construed as a process: it can never
be satisfied for more than an instant and it has to be continually reenacted. It drives people unremittingly.

The world works at least one trick on the masculine character in Lacan's drama of Oedipus. The impulse of conquest
that seems so self-assertive can also be interpreted as craven
or behoven to unmanageable attractions. A masculine subject
doesn't necessarily push where it thinks it desires. Rather, as
Paul Virilio has suggested, a system of "seduction" operates
even though the masculine character might think of itself as
the initiator: "The leading aside *(seducere)* of seduction, then
is inscribed very precisely in the dynamic of the world; there
woman is not possessive, possessed or possessing, but attractive. This force of attraction is in fact gravitation, universal
heaviness. The *axis mundi*. Mistress of passage, she has up till
now effectively organized all that is speed."[2]

If the Oedipus story is one of the mythic fundamentals
of Western society, Genesis would have to be another. If Oedipus dramatizes the institution of personalities in society, Genesis plays out what happens when a subject tries to *move*, to
act socially. As Virilio notes, the feminine is accorded responsibility (or blame) for all such movement. The Fall, he says,
is the definitive impetus of Western society: "seduction here
takes on a cosmo-dynamic dimension; seduction is a rite of
passage from one universe to another." The paradox is that
The Fall enables us to be social beings, it enables us to be
human: this is the attraction of the story. Hence European

writers through the ages have celebrated that "*happy* fruit whereof our first parents Adam and Eve tasted, whereby they lost their felicities and procured death to them and their posteritie."[3] The loss of elemental felicity means that *human* action has become feasible; The Fall brings human society into being. The catch is that the "happy fruit" is gone once The Fall occurs, and after that the ruling symbol, the *signifier*, in the Fallen society is the talisman of the phallus. How to *possess* it? How to *become* it? If action is to occur in the orthodox world of men and women, it happens after the disposal of the happy fruit of equable sociability. It cannot be had and eaten too. Wherever there is action, occupation, or enterprise, there is a subject asserting itself in the objective world, and there is, therefore, contestation between complexes of masculinity and feminity. The dialectic may not always be explicit. Virilio explains in his own dramatic terms by concentrating on the fate of the feminine principle: "Little by little the tragic character of the necessity to seduce and to keep on seducing is revealed: it is like an exorbitant inflation of the law of movement and the vectoral faculties of the body, like an acceleration of the irresistible disappearance of the partner or partners in space and time: to lead them aside is to lead them to nothingness."[4]

And here in the late twentieth century such a dynamic between the masculine and the feminine is evidently still tragic and is probably leading nowhere. What have been its costs in the past? Everyone could refer to private remembrances to find some answers. But I want to examine the national past. A history of Western subjectivity can be charted across the two centuries of white Australia. This continent, how has she been occupied?

II. Precipitation

Two centuries of white Australia? Certainly it is misleading to begin the English story with Captain Cook or Governor Phillip. The Antipodes—a mirror to European aspirations and anxieties—had been projected since antiquity. There was never much doubt that a territory would finally be located to fit the map. Long before the English discovery, the Southern Continent was being written into Western culture.

The year 1788 is simply when the first *visible* marks of European culture were scored here: for a brief time everything seemed "infantile" again. David Collins disembarked from the First Fleet and waited for some kind of communal identity to emerge from the seeming perversity.

> The confusion that ensued will not be wondered at when it is considered that every man stepped from the boat literally into a wood . . . the spot which had so lately been the abode of silence and tranquility was now changed to that of noise, clamour, and confusion: but after a time order gradually prevailed every where. As the woods were opened and the ground cleared, the various encampments were extended, and all wore the appearance of regularity.[5]

Given no other choice, they set about living in what seemed to them to be this "other" land.

The Britons living in Governor Phillip's Australia were confronted by what they construed to be "unwrought Nature." The continent could not be addressed and made sensible until it was incorporated into Culture. Indeed, the comprehension of Australia as Nature was the principal action of this incorporation. The continent was called an empty page, and stories and systems were thus made ready to be set down on it.

The society required a relationship with the land. Like the infant written into the symbolic order, so nature was given over to culture. Speech in the infancy of white Australia was tolerated from a select caste, which was English, scientific, military, acquisitive, and male. By dint of attrition, resistant groups were outlasted; it was not bloodless or conciliatory, but it was a comprehensive takeover in the long run. (To detail the accession of English significance is to delineate a willful ignorance of Aboriginal inscriptions on the land. White Australian history must be seen now as a palimpsest; the underlying autochthonous scriptures are emerging ever more insistently.)

So Oedipus came to the Antipodes, not in banishment, not in debasement, but full of influence. During the infancy of white Australia, a tyranny of difference began to reign. The pioneer-subject looked out and saw Mother Nature and sought to reunite himself with her. He had to possess her and incorporate her. So the conquistadorial process was instigated. The Blue Mountains were "penetrated" (the word appears repeatedly in explorers' journals), and heroic energies were expended into one of the last great Other Worlds of Earth—the Outback.

More than a century before Patrick White's Voss declaimed, "I am compelled into this country," Thomas Mitchell had profited from the compulsion and accounted for himself with reference to one of the fundamental myths: "We had at length discovered a country ready for the immediate reception of civilised man, and fit to become eventually one of the great nations of the earth. . . . Of this Eden it seemed I was the only Adam; and it was indeed a sort of paradise to me."[6]

The explorer is Adam. But where is Eve? It seems plausi-

ble to say she is the landscape herself. In a masculinist orthodoxy such as the explorers' code the geographical space is in
place to be possessed, to be entered and incorporated by the
hero. Moreover, the land is *attractive*.

Charles Sturt corroborates when he offers his personal
history of Australian geography in terms of a subliminal drama
of divestment: "The further knowledge that has been gained
of the interior is but as a gleam of sunshine over an extensive
landscape. A stronger light has fallen upon the nearer ground,
but the distant horizon is still enveloped in clouds. The veil
has only as it were been withdrawn from the marshes of the
Macquarie, to be spread over the channel of the Darling."[7]
And still more revealing is Sturt's reference to the geometric
center of the continent: "Men of undoubted perseverance and
energy had tried to work their way to that distant and
shrouded spot. A veil hung over Central Australia that could
neither be pierced nor raised. Girt around by deserts, it almost
appeared as if Nature had intentionally closed it upon civilised
man, that she might have one domain on earth's wide field
over which the savage might roam in freedom."[8] In Virilio's
terms, the explorer is led aside into nothingness. But there
is always one region that remains "savage," "feminine,"
"other."

This is a mythological ploy which explains away the im-
plausibility of the quest to reify the entire continent in terms
of its submissiveness and bounty. The explorer is led aside,
over the horizon, but once there the promised land is void
and a new, unbroached horizon beckons. The logical conclusion is to learn from disappointment and to abjure the quest.
The *mythological* solution is to render the secular failure as a
spiritual triumph—a transcendental confirmation of the nobil-
ity and vitality of the quest. There is something sacred about

such conquistadorial aspirations, even when they are repeatedly thwarted. The explorer senses he is being seduced and he accepts the intrigue, as Sturt testifies when he reflects on his fortunes in exploring southern Australia: "It almost appeared as if Nature had resisted us in order to try our perseverance, and that she had yielded in pity to our efforts."[9]

Nowadays the explorers come in different guises, but the actions and motivations are often similar, and the landscape is still seductive for men of action with the right stuff for the contest. The choreography of moves in the sexual orientation of a nationalist culture follows many of the same patterns. The most potent characters would be defined as those most able to occupy territory. Space is still the object being reified, but the technology which best facilitates territorial occupancy of territory becomes the most fervently sought after commodity. A vehicle can thus become a fetish, embodying all the complex desires for spatial ubiquity or potency. A car, a ship, a horse, or a plane might take on a sweetheart's name. For Mitchell, Eve may have been embodied in the landscape of Eden, but for the modern proprietor of a nation, the phallus might now be had in the form of appliances and technological hardware, mysterious, seductive, and definitive of a man's dominion in the modern territory. The explorer might now appear as the satellite-communications engineer at North-West Cape, the fighter pilot cruising over Port Douglas, Donald Campbell on the Lake Eyre saltpan, or the American on the subterranean console at Pine Gap.

Finally, it is still the same sad vertigo of seduction, because the technology merely delays the evaporation of the desired object at the instant of seeming possession. At the limit of acceleration or programming, the world still outstrips any single subjective authority brought to bear upon it. Because the technology available is still prosthetic rather than genetic, it does not change the nature of the objective world. Available technology is still only a tool rather than a miracle. At this stage it simply alters the conditions of access operating between a subject and an object. At terminal velocity (of missiles, Mirages, or messages), the world which seemed so mutable during acceleration appears again to be unchanged, and the possession of space (for example) must be acknowledged as a futile project because there is no longer any possibility of deluding oneself that one can move even faster, constantly approaching that state of ubiquity which would be ultimate spatial possession. There is a myth to explain this aspect of masculinity too—the story of Icarus.

At terminal velocity the landscape slips away again, unpossessed. Indeed, Sturt learned his Icaran lessons and attempted to redefine himself and his quests. He had reached a stasis that can be understood as something like terminal velocity during their intracontinental treks. He found himself trudging space that was, subjectively speaking, virtually unmeasurable and invariable for them as he attempted to forge into the environment in order to take possession of it. He wrote an account of being effectively frozen in stillness, unable to feel like a subject in control of a Nature which ought to be compliant to a conquistador ranging over his vanquished domain.

Sturt finally took the more humble option. But this is not to say that everyone has redefined their understanding of their place in the landscape. The more militarist attitude, which sees the continent as a foe to be brought to rule, still ranges abroad. The submerged domes of Pine Gap are obvious talismans: white Australians' (mythically induced) sense of the untouchability of the geographical center has been turned to military advantage: what better place to locate unknowable technology than the arcane heartland where Nature preserves the most occult of mysteries? It is a canny ploy. Whereas white Australia has traditionally looked for security *from* the landscape, a black magic promises to turn the world upside down by maintaining that there is security *in* the landscape. It appears to be a new relationship to the environment, but it is actually an extension of our alienation from it. When the land becomes so otherworldly that only a "masonic" class of technocrats can administer it, the conquistadorial class has taken its project to its endpoint, back to a feudal model of society and the universe wherein the majority of citizens might exist in vassalage so long as it believes that the technocratic class knows the secrets that have been occulted.

This is a powerful trick that is worked through storytelling, and it can succeed so long as the audience is willing to suspend its disbelief. What if the citizenry declined to believe in the quest to subdue Eden?

5

Beyond the Compass of Words

Edgar Allan Poe, the South Seas, and "A Manuscript Found in a Bottle"

I have reached these lands but newly
From an ultimate dim Thule—
From a wild weird clime that lieth, sublime,
Out of Space—out of Time.

      E. A. Poe, "Dream-Land" (1844)

The 1830s: all through the South Pacific, the myriad islands are being located and turned to profit or virtue by fleets of Western speculators; missionaries secure souls for Christendom; whalers take stock enroute to colder climes; sandalwood traders cull the island hillsides and set sail for Shanghai, laden with aromatic cargo that smells like prestige to the Oriental, but has the whiff of money for the Occidental. Either way, from East or West, the South already has a shape, a fragrance, and a color.

Due west of the "balmy islands," it is now three decades since Matthew Flinders has girt the New Holland coastline with meticulous survey, thereby staking out one of the last geographical enigmas and earning the right to proffer a name for the continent—Australia: Definitive South. So, the colony receives its connotations. Not only is it redolent with a criminal stench, but it is also imbued with Southernness, a potpourri of novelty, profit, luxuriance, and futurity.

In America, meanwhile, the sea change has commenced which will eventually tarnish the ideals of Revolutionary America, sending microcosmic craft like Ahab's "Pequod" (Herman Melville, *Moby-Dick,* 1851) and Huck and Jim's raft (Mark Twain, *The Adventures of Huckleberry Finn,* 1884) adrift on waters of a melancholy, but persistent utopian yearning, waters eddying away from a New World which has become less than dreamlike.

1833: Edgar Allan Poe senses the winds of change and impels them a little by publishing the first of his maritime stories, "A MS. Found in a Bottle."[1] It is a tale in which everything eventually succumbs to the attraction of Legendary South, which is a place, an idea, and a climactic event in the story. The South, as Poe imagines it, is dense with a European mythology that shapes the histories of the region as English, French, American, and white Australian navigators quantify and occupy the Pacific and its land masses.

As Poe woke begrudgingly from the dream of America, he looked to the South Seas and discerned a world of fantasy that was just beginning to be realized. At this moment of Western history, therefore, the South seemed ready-made as a site for Poe's musings about Utopia, beauty, evil, and chaos. The South seemed the ideal place to locate a story that was both fantastic and referential. The writer could conjure a society beyond known experience and, at the same time, he could ponder the beliefs and shortfalls of his American reality. In the idea of the South Seas, Poe found the setting for a story that was to be neither entirely "vaporous" like fable, nor speciously substantial like empiricism—neither myth nor history, but something on the cusp of the two. But what previous references gave Poe his Southern bearings? How did he arrive in such waters?

Two of his favorite authors—Daniel Defoe and Jonathan Swift[2]—had plotted the legendary hemisphere before him. In *Captain Singleton* (1720) and *A New Voyage round the World* (1725), Defoe depicted the South Pacific in a terse, observational prose whose seeming veracity was reinforced by navigational and experiential references grafted from mariners' logbooks (most notably from the records of William Dampier). This was imaginative writing which sought to minimize its sense of originality. It was a fantastic tale rendered in the most "responsible" prose; it was the stuff of paradox. Within his outwardly sober books, Defoe detailed a world of maritime toil and tedium, yet he also described diverting sojourns in a fictional South of opulence and sensual indulgence.

To similar effect, Swift imagined the islands of Blefuscu, Lilliput, and Houyhnhnm-Land inside the bounds of sketchy contemporary maps of New Holland. Within a world that could now be empirically charted, it was still possible to locate one's imaginative projections. Such was the topography of a "fantastically real" South.

Both Swift and Defoe were producing a "twilight" kind of fiction involving imagined societies placed with cartographic precision in a habitable setting far from the foibles of established Western societies. Whether these tales are utopian or dystopian is a moot point, but they are fictions of a "New World": they are critical fictions reflecting indirectly on real conditions in the mundane worlds of the West. They use the

South for their speculation, and in the process they embellish an image of the planet's nether regions as a realm of mystique and other-worldliness.

Moreover, in addition to the influences of these two "inspirational" precursors, Poe was well schooled in the deeper traditions of austral writing. Indeed, he was student enough to follow such narratives not only through the journals of Captains Cook and Briscoe and in the voyage anthologies of Archibald Dunn (1806) and Benjamin Morrell (1832), but also into the esoteric conjectures of John Cleves Symmes and Jeremiah Reynolds who, at least until 1829, maintained that a temperate, fecund region existed inside the earth's shell on an inverted continental shelf supposedly formed by an enormous antarctic maelstrom.[3]

Accordingly, when Poe commences his "A MS. Found in a Bottle" at Batavia, "in the year 18——,"[4] setting his mariners' course "S.E. by S." to "run down the coast of New Holland" (note the archaic, pre-Flinders name which fixes the setting in a time outside the present), he knows the tale is bound for shifting grounds that are half-surveyed and half-projected, half palpable and half nebulous, half historical and half mythical. He is contributing to the austral tradition of English literature.

But, before following this drift, we might pause to ask why such a voyage should interest us here and now. This is a question about what it means to live in the South Land of European and American Imagining. The custom of envisaging Geographic South as an ambivalently beckoning locale has undoubtedly influenced the European communities that have developed in the austral region (to the detriment of the indigenes, it must be affirmed immediately). An examination of

Southern narratives might help us plumb the complex idealist current that flows through colonial cultures in the South Pacific region. We might understand better how, repeatedly, a utopian mythology has provided both a map and an alibi for a mercantile history of usurpation and exploitation by European cultures and economies in the region.

As Ernst Cassirer has indicated, history is generally *prefigured* rather than recounted: "In the relation between myth and history myth proves to be the primary, history the secondary and derived, factor. It is not by its history that the mythology of a nation is determined but, conversely, its history is determined by its mythology—or rather the mythology of a people does not *determine* but *is* its fate, its destiny as decreed from the very beginning."[5] By looking back to some of the promotional myths that gave rise to white societies in the South Pacific, we might understand more subtly some of the fantasies that still animate political life in a nation such as Australia. For example, we might understand a little better, in retrospect, the extraordinary effectiveness of Bob Hawke's rhetoric during the early 1980s, before the conviction behind the words had been tested.

How to evaluate the panache and the effectiveness of the prospective Prime Minister's performances in February 1983? The candidate looks up, pauses, his voice about to crack. "This is a fight for the future of Australia, for the true heart and soul of Australia," he declares. It's a fight to "win our way through the crises into which the policies of the past and the men of the past have plunged our country."[6] Perhaps we can see now how these myths of the New Worlds in contest with Old Worlds served to "naturalize" a system of progressive colonization: internally, white Australia certified itself as legitimate by hearkening to a creed of developmentalism; externally "greater" powers continued to perceive the Pacific region as ripe for the picking, as the region of the future.

But we have been drifting: in "A MS. Found in a Bottle," Poe's protagonist embarks for the South Seas, in quest of thematic twilight. On the evidence of this story, Poe is fascinated by terror and the altered consciousness it can induce, and he thrills to the "alchemic" qualities of language, whereby words can represent worlds and feelings even as chaos or ignorance threatens.

But more perversely (and typically of Poe), he is especially charmed by situations in which sense will not hold, and anxiety abounds. Through the agency of a narrator who is animated by an uneasy desire for subjective motility, Poe will use the mariner's tale to chart the dim tracts of subjective experience where words dry up and where language cannot be summonsed to invoke, evoke, or explain. He will use this South Seas yarn to tell of a real world at its unrealizable or unspeakable limits.

Such subjective brinkmanship will become an abiding concern for Poe throughout his writing career. In *The Narrative of Arthur Gordon Pym* (1837), he will extol the purity of mind consequent to being "resuscitated from a state bordering very nearly upon death"; in "Ligeia" (1838) he will ponder the state of being "upon the very verge of remembrance, without being able, in the end, to remember"; and in "The Facts in the Case of M. Valdemar" (1845) he will concoct a convincing "scientific" case study of a living/dead, a man "mesmerised *in articulo mortis*."

In one of his "minor" pieces, from the *Marginalia*, Poe analyzes his obsession with these states of suspension. Crucially, he indicates that the fascination is linguistic:

How very commonly we hear it remarked, that such and such thoughts are beyond the compass of words! I do not believe that any thought, properly so called, is out of the reach of language. I fancy, rather, that where difficulty of expression is experienced, there is, in the intellect which experiences it, a want either of deliberateness or method. There is, however, a class of fancies of exquisite delicacy, which are *not* thoughts, and to which, *as yet*, I have found it absolutely impossible to adapt language. . . . They seem to me rather psychal than intellectual. They arise from the soul (alas, how rarely!) only at its epochs of most intense tranquillity—when the bodily and mental health are in perfection—and those mere points of time where the confines of the waking world blend with those of the world of dreams. I am aware of these "fancies" only when I am upon the very brink of sleep. . . .[7]

One cannot ascribe a proper name to these "psychal" phenomena. A *thought* can be described or presented linguistically; but these phenomena are something else. They happen in muteness. They cannot be rendered empirically or made to fit an existent taxonomy. In the context of Poe's times, they are "monstrous" inasmuch as they cannot be accommodated by a scientific worldview or by a nominalist model of language. But it is typical of Poe that he is attracted to the monsters, and he suspects that they can be known, or "sensed" perhaps, by *approaching*, rather than accommodating, them with language. If phenomena beyond the compass of words cannot be comprehensively described or presented, they can be *evoked*; one can gesture meaningfully toward them. One can attest to their existence and account for the context in which they occur, and one can *imagine* around them even if they cannot be named.[8]

Because the investigation of such "monstrosity" requires

a melodramatic setting, a setting which is recognizable in realist terms but which also oversteps the restraint of realist decorums, it was a South Seas tale that Poe chose as the form for approaching such a theme. Moreover, the South Seas tales is generically utopian: traditionally, it is a dreamer's form. And for all his perversity, Poe is habitually utopian, not in a politically programmatic way, but because of his ineluctable desire for self-abnegation or self-transcendence, because of his desire to move elsewhere subjectively. It seems almost inevitable, therefore, that Poe would be drawn early in his career to utilize *and embellish* the West's image of the South.

In "A MS Found in a Bottle" Poe gave form to his themes of enunciative suspension so thoroughly that the story is twilighted in formal as well as thematic terms. As Donald Stauffer notes, "the tale is written in two quite different styles, to which we might apply the terms 'plausible' and 'arabesque'," and it is the "interweaving of these two styles, one of which predominates at the beginning and the other at the end" that gives the story its "texture of mixed fact and fantasy."[9] Of course, it is an American manuscript that Poe presents, but, in a particular sense, it is also an austral one.

The story begins in the environs of memory, with the narrator attempting to trace through his past in order to draw sense from a present predicament which assails him even as he reminisces. While he writes, he recalls that he was once the personification of objectivity and mental order; he was blessed with a "contemplative turn of mind which enabled [him] to methodise the stores which early study very diligently garnered up" [p. 99]. But, he recalls, this competence and stability gave him no peace. He sensed in himself "a kind of nervous restlessness which haunted [him] as a fiend" [p. 100]. His peripatetic anxiety led him to Java, where he embarked on an unnamed ship bound S.S.E.

Still bringing the tale through recent memory, approaching the protagonist-writer's present tense, the manuscript recounts how the days passed in routine until, one evening, a change of weather blew in. As the text describes this turn of events, the language of the reminiscence undergoes a significant atmospheric adjustment. Up to this stage the prose style has been deliberately naturalistic—observational and metonymic, virtually devoid of evocative epithets. Thus far, words and things have seemed to correspond, one to another, in stable objective duplication, with reference and referents being coupled in the equable service of description. For example: "Our vessel was a beautiful ship of about four hundred tons, copper-fastened and built at Bombay of Malabar teak. She was freighted with cotton-wool and oil, from the Lachadive islands. We also had on board coir, jaggaree, ghee, cocoa-nuts, and a few cases of opium. The stowage was clumsily done, and the vessel consequently crank" [p. 100]. Prior to the sea change that we are about to notice, the narrator has been able to observe a *knowable* world, where each object has been discrete, describable, and specific. Each effect has been easily attributable to a cause.

But once the atmosphere alters, the world cannot be so comfortably figured. The narrator records how evening lowered, and the ship was becalmed. He remembers a "full presentiment of evil," which he conjures now with pathetic fallacy, a trope heretofore foreign to the prose style: the moon flushes "dusky-red" and the air becomes intolerably hot and is festooned with "spiral exhalations similar to those arising from heated iron" [p. 100]. The prose begins to wax metaphorical.

"A wilderness of foam" howls in, the ship is wrenched from its placidity, and the language is regaled with epithet and assonance: the rigging tears "like pack-thread," the sun takes on a "sickly yellow lustre" as it "clambers" above the horizon, and, in a deft synaesthetic touch, Poe intones the prose with viscous open vowels and tolling double *L*s to describe the thick and heavy dusk as a "dull and sullen glow without reflection" [p. 102].

At this juncture, the ship is propelled, "at a rate defying computation" [p. 102], away from empirical certainties. And the prose that comprises the tale is also hauled away from the surety of metonymic, naturalist description into the chartless areas of poetic evocation, away from the realm of "thoughts," perhaps, and toward Poe's state of evanescent "fancies."

Needless to say, the narrator's "methodized" intellect is somewhat blustered by now. With the tale progressing, he traces back through more recent memory, leading us toward the last instance of his intelligibility, just before the manuscript went into the bottle, the last instance when language was unable to cover, or even approach, the event, the instant at the end of the story, when writing must stop.

But he is not there yet. The ship careers on, into a region heavy with metaphor. All around is "horror, thick gloom, and a black sweltering desert of ebony" [p. 103]. The sense of composure that had initially characterized both the narrator and the voyage has been dispelled. The ship can be brought under no human influence, and the once-voluble and erudite narrator is struck dumb, "wrapped up in silent wonder," as he stares "bitterly into the world of ocean." He has become a vagrant in a world with no reliable references, no names, no categories or calibrations. A world of negation: "we had no means of calculating time, nor could we form any guess of our situation.

We were, however, well aware of having made farther to the southward than any previous navigators" [p. 103].

Here in austral regions, where history and myth commingle, naturalistic description can barely communicate the experience. The narrator has arrived at the limits of comprehensible subjectivity: "I could not help feeling the utter hopelessness of hope itself, and prepared myself gloomily for that death which I thought nothing could defer for beyond an hour" [p. 103]. But then, through the agency of terror in this instance, rather than through the somnolence or mesmerism Poe describes in the *Marginalia*, the narrator enters an existential state beyond words or thoughts, a feeling of psychal lucidity: "I know not what sudden self-possession came over my spirit. . . . I awaited fearlessly the ruin that was to overwhelm" [p. 104].

At this instant, when the empirical world has been left behind, the ship collides with a mass of legend. A huge ghost ship, a variant of the mythical Flying Dutchman, looms out of nowhere, obliterating the original vessel, catapulting the narrator into the air, and ensnaring him in the new craft's towering, antique rigging.

Now he is borne southward in a fabulous vehicle which will be both his salvation and his nemesis. The new ship sails on, through experiences that words cannot shadow:

> A feeling, for which I have no name, has taken possession of my soul—a sensation that will admit of no analysis, to which the lessons of bygone times are inadequate, and for which I fear futurity itself will offer me no key. To a mind constituted like my own, the latter consideration is an evil. I shall never—I know that I shall never—be satisfied with regard to the nature of my conceptions [p. 105].

Here are phenomena which cannot be fitted to a rational scheme. The narrator finds himself confronted with sublimity, a set of impressions that outstrip his systems of comprehension and representation, and he cannot find it beautiful or transcendent (as Kantian aesthetics would): rather, he finds it evil.

Poe's narrator hails from a skeptical age, when political programs for futurity, scientific discoveries about the workings of the world, and rational criteria of evaluation were all on trial in "courts" of Romantic aesthetics and social theory. Stanley Cavell has developed an interpretation of Romanticism which is helpful in coming to terms with Poe's self-abnegating perversity. Cavell contends that Romanticism must be construed to be "working out a crisis of knowledge, a crisis I have characterised as . . . a response at once to the threat of skepticism and to a disappointment with philosophy's answer to this threat, particularly as embodied in the achievement of Kant's philosophy." Romanticism thus arises out of a challenge, "the task of bringing the world back, as to life. This may in turn present itself as the quest for a return to the ordinary, or of it, a new creation of our habitat; or as a quest, away from that, for the creation of a new inhabitation."[10]

Poe is preoccupied, therefore, with surveying "the new inhabitation." Certainly, he does not crave a "return of the ordinary" through the retrieval of an untraumatized sense of serenity or beauty. Rather, he wants to admit evil, quite literally to admit it into his comprehension of the world, to confront mortifying experience and to bring himself back to life without denying that he is now aware of some things that cannot be thought. In another essay it might be argued that the new inhabitation Poe was surveying is the unconscious. But for now, I'd rather stay within manageable argumentative limits and restrict the inquest to aesthetics and linguistics, to see how Poe invoked the image of the South to communicate his attitudes about what might be thinkable and speakable in his era of skepticism.

Once the narrator of the "MS." is hurled into the ghost ship, the tale is plotted southward into realms outside the latitudes of goodness, beauty, and recorded or "civilized" experience. The lessons of bygone times now seem inadequate. The narrator's former sense of decorum is bound to be hexed.

As the tale struggles to tell, the ship slides down the globe, and the days pass by in darkness. Only once is there a glimmer of explanation, as the craft is drawn inexorably southward: recalling how he was one day lost in reverie, "musing upon the singularity of [his] fate," the protagonist tells how he "unwittingly daubed with a tar-brush the edges of a neatly folded studding-sail" that was lying on the deck; when the sail is run up the mast, it unfurls in propulsion, and the narrator looks up to see that "the thoughtless touches of the brush are spread out in the word DISCOVERY" [p. 106].

Perhaps it is the spirit of monstrosity in the air or perhaps it is the unconscious that has placed the heraldic word in the rigging high above the southbound craft. Regardless of where the fanciful notion has sprung from, the crucial point is that at this "thoughtless" stage, the narrative catches up with the narrator. The "MS." is no longer enunciated as reminiscence; from now on in the manuscript, the writing is contemporaneous with, and complicit in, the events being represented. The writing is now utterly present, foregrounded as a dramatic event, emphasized as the rigging of any meaning which may arise.

As he attempts to record his perceptions of objects and occurrences which he finds indescribable, the narrator utilizes language which, he admits, cannot denote everything that he wishes to represent. As *fancies* proliferate, he continues to present his *thoughts*, in the hope that he might be able to evoke something more than the flimsy framework of rationality that his language can construct. But outside the world of intelligible language, he senses something compelling and disconcerting: "A new sense—a new entity is added to my soul" [p. 105]. As he writes, he "hovers continually on the brink of eternity, without taking a final plunge into the abyss" [p. 107]. In such a state of subjective distension, his writing is forced back to the basics, back to the binary process of a myriad negations through which the naming of specific objects is possible. The narrator begins an infantile process of contextualizing and comprehending the ship: "What she *is not*, I can easily perceive—what she *is* I fear it is impossible to say" [p. 106]. In this realm of new experience, the narrator yearns for new and unfamiliar words; he craves invention.

And still the ship gravitates "due south . . . into the most appalling hell of water it can enter the mind of man to imagine" [p. 107], through a "chaos of foamless water" amidst "stupendous ramparts of ice . . . looking like the walls of the universe" [p. 109]. And as if to emphasize that he is now in a realm beyond thought, where rational decorum is not observed and fancies seep through, where "words are trivial and ineffective" [p. 108], the narrator takes time to scrutinize the comportment of the phantom crew. "The ship and all in it are imbued with the spirit of eld," he observes. The sailors "glide to and fro like the ghosts of buried centuries," and the captain, the embodiment of Old World authority, scrabbles for direction in this world of novelty, ineffectually referring to his "mouldering instruments of science and obsolete, long-forgotten charts" [pp. 108–109].

There can be no doubting that the craft is heading for

the region of the unpresentable. Yet, in keeping with Poe's conception of Mythologic South as a realm of possibility as well as potential terror, the crew do not appear irretrievably lost: "there is upon their countenances an expression more of the eagerness of hope than of the apathy of despair" [p. 109]. True to Poe's Romantic creed of brinkmanship (and attuned perhaps to Goethe's maxim, "Die, and become"), there is a sense of possibility suffusing the atmosphere of abjection. Just before the ship plunges into the antarctic maelstrom, the narrator's mood becomes paradoxically buoyant:

> To conceive the horror of my sensations is, I presume, utterly impossible; yet a curiosity to penetrate the mysteries of these awful regions, predominates even over my despair, and will reconcile me to the most hideous aspect of death. It is evident that we are hurrying onwards to some exciting knowledge—some never-to-be-imparted secret, whose attainment is destruction [p. 109].

Moments after this note of metaphysical ambition, the narrator must cast the manuscript to futurity. This is where writing must stop. But it may also be where other experiences can be *sensed* even though they may not yet have been methodized in language. When the narrator balks at naming or describing an experience, he has arrived at the endpoint of a programmatic quest for "extra-systemic" knowledge.

Such a "transcendental" conclusion to the tale emphasizes how "A MS. Found in a Bottle" can be read as dynamically mythical (in Cassirer's sense) with regard to the story's exploitation and elaboration of orthodox European notions about the South Seas. For, the austral utopian tradition can be described as a set of myths about the rejection of old worldviews, myths about moments of social or subjective disorder in which the unachieved or even the unimagined might be glimpsed or perhaps enacted.

Indeed, one could argue that the austral utopian tradition is the communal (or mythic) dimension of the Western individual's desire for self-transcendence. Charles Baudelaire observed that "in Poe's stories, love does not speak its name."[11] With this contention in mind, one might interpret Poe's preoccupation with those verges "beyond the compass of words" as an abiding urge to disintegrate his self in order to inhabit a changed and better future. Such a desire can be presented on the most personal scale, of course. But the fascinating aspect about "A MS. Found in a Bottle" is the mythic or social dimension of allegory that Poe writes into the narrative. Where did he take the idea of Mythologic South, and where did it take him?

Given the traditions of austral writing and subjective brinkmanship that Poe was manipulating, the linguistic form of the "MS." is perfectly suited to conjoining the psychic and the social themes of the story. Poe's writing does not tamper spectacularly with language in the way that, say, James Joyce *presents* a state beyond law-abiding language and social decorum in *Finnegans Wake*. Poe chooses, rather, to *suggest* such a state stylistically. Note, for example, the "intemperate" adjectival lyricism that gradually "contaminates," but never completely destabilizes, the observational writing which prevailed at the beginning of the text. The narrator repeatedly *refers* to a state of subjective abandon, but he never attempts a verbal presentation of the linguistic void. Poe does not wish to run the risk of losing sense altogether. He wants, rather to gesture toward possibilities not yet realized subjectively, socially, or linguistically. He implies that one needs a basis in the ordinary in order to get a sense of the extraordinary.

Poe resolves to stay within the bounds of conventionally composed language even as he affirms the existence of an alluring world just beyond the semantic horizon. Taking the South Seas as his setting, he contrives to write in an evanescent manner so that his prose tends toward, but stops short of, decomposition. He does not finally unsettle the illusion of reference in his language. His words still purport to be *about* the South Seas and the mariner's experiences there, rather than being *words about words* (as might be argued for Joyce's modernist classics). As part of the contract of willing suspension of disbelief between writer and reader, the setting and the events encountered in the story refer to a reality in a world that outreaches the first and last page of the manuscript. Yet that part of the larger world, that Southern referent, is also unequivocally described as fantastic. Such is the dual nature of the South Seas in nineteenth-century writing. This is not to say something as simplistic as Poe's story is about the real world, while *Finnegans Wake* is about language. There can be no separating the world and language—each is part of the other. But certainly Poe was concerned to illuminate the twilight world between geographical actuality (describable in received language) and the fantastic, but nonetheless real, history of utopian yearning and discovery in Western culture.

In order to discover, one must start from what is known and comprehensible, and in stylistic terms Poe stays just inside these significant limits. However, prior to discovery, one also needs a sense of what one is looking for. In choosing as his setting the half-documented, half-imagined South Seas which antiquity had invested with so much ambiguous promise, Poe ensured that his tale could be about the impulse to marry the creative possibilities of mythological composition with the mundanities of lived experience. In short, he chose the setting which would allow him to drift with the utopian current that so often flows in the gulf between myth and history.

And because Southern myths such as Poe's (and Swift's, Defoe's, Dampier's, Augustine's, Ptolemy's . . .) have contributed to Southern histories, it is vital nowadays to examine the stories so we can discover some of the patterns that construct a populace.

6

The Keen Historic Spasm

Rhetorical Uses for the Archival Photograph

Early in Walker Evans's and James Agee's *Let Us Now Praise Famous Men* there is a pulse-quickening sequence in which Agee describes lovingly the dramatic vigil endured and enjoyed as Evans awaits the perfect moment to *take a picture*, literally to take it out of the evanescent world of time. Agee and Evans have been out driving the dirt roads of Alabama when they negotiate a curve and are presented with a simple wooden church testifying to some significant but unspeakable "goodness" as it stands in the "serene, wild, rigorous light." Simultaneously both men mutter an awestruck "Jesus" before Agee brakes hard and backs up the car to the roadside so they can ponder and perhaps give form to what struck them both so piquantly. They set up the camera and watch as the sun subtly changes. The church "stood empty in the meditation of the sun: and this light upon it was strengthening still further its imposal and embrace, and in about a quarter of an hour would have trained itself ready, and there would be a triple convergence in the keen historic spasm of the shutter."[1]

This sequence is impressive not only because of the orotund grandeur of Agee's prose, but also because of the pacing of the story—the rhythm of retention and divulgence of information syncopated to a sense of temporal urgency in the capricious sunlight. In this passage, in which Agee needs to establish some fundamental tenets of his photographic aesthetic, he chooses to tell a story—he chooses to convince the reader by narrating rather than by simply declaiming. He is aware that a photograph cannot be understood without a yarn being spun about it. When the shutter scythes back and forth, history is in the making, a set of data is scooped out of temporal experience and stored for use after the moment of the spasm. This is the instant of the "triple convergence," the barely perceptible event which he describes in the next paragraph as a moment when something is "trapped, possessed, fertilized." These three factors define for Agee (and for me and this essay) the historic nature of a photo: a momentary action is arrested and stored, but, crucially, it is also primed to grow.

The Oxford English Dictionary also works in triplicate when dealing with history, when it presents the Greek root *historia* as meaning, simultaneously and somewhat obliquely, "finding out" and "narrative" as well as the direct translation, "history." After the O.E.D. has broken the word into its base parts, it is informative to integrate those parts again. Finding out how to narrate a story that gets accepted as history—this is how I would like to define the historiographical use of the photograph.

This may seem an unsurprising definition. Obviously, a photograph needs to be considered in the context either of the time and place of its original configuration or in the circumstances of its redeployment. Which is to say, once captured and stored, the image is reinserted (regrafted? refertilized?) in a culture of events, aspirations, and actions. This would seem obvious. However, the complexities of managing the germination and ramifications of any one photograph have not been thoroughly theorized. Furthermore, in many professions and disciplines which rely heavily on the interpretation of photographic images, there is ignorance or disregard of the significance of the narrative component of the picture. For example, in the discipline of anthropology, many theorists and practitioners ignore the narrative potential of the image when they attempt to "put it to use." In a highly influential anthology on visual anthropology, John Collier suggests that: "Photography's contributions to anthropology lie in three basic areas: Ray Birdwhistell's 'kinesics,' the significance of body expression; Edward T. Hall's 'proxemics,' the meaning of space in human behaviour; and Alan Lomax's 'choreometrics,' the choreography of culture."[2]

Although the notion of "choreometrics" does imply a sense of duration and ongoing relations among people and things, there is very little to suggest that narrative, as a form of knowledge construction and communication, is taken seriously within Collier's operations. Collier's attention to photography entails a triple convergence of one kind, but it is not commensurate with Agee's. When Collier redefines photography's utility in terms of how it enables the anthropologist "to MEASURE, to COUNT, and to COMPARE,"[3] his triad lines up with only two of Agee's points of convergence: Collier acknowledges the way a photograph "traps" and "possesses," but the "fertility" of the image is not explicitly acknowledged even though, invariably, a discourse—an essay, a lecture, or an argument with conclusions—will be developed out of the picture by the anthropologist.

Field reports are tales recollected and composed in the "tranquillity" of tents, aircraft, studies—in spaces and times removed from the instant of observation—and are interpretations of collected data. Indeed, the collection of the data has already proceeded, consciously or unconsciously, through selection, exemption, and combination in the instant of recording. This proposition, that evidence is already shaped subjectively precisely because it has been called evidence, serves to emphasize the mythic or narrative potential inherent to ethnographic photography—the photo has been taken and has been used as evidence so that the ethnographic interpretation may proceed.

The subjectivity of such disciplined storytelling (so "disciplined" that it rarely calls itself storytelling) has only recently been seriously examined, in the anthropological/textual criticism of James Clifford, for example.[4] In due course, I will examine more thoroughly the question of the latent narrativity of the photographic image with reference to historiographical concerns. For the moment let me simply speculate that the controversies around anthropological uses of photography are pertinent, also, to historical research. If one accepts that the past can indeed be regarded as another country, then the people pictured there confront us with the characteristics of an exotic, arcane race.

But in order to proceed, let me state simplistically what I mean by the storytelling potential of photography. I mean, quite blatantly, the potential to use or exploit a photograph for the purposes of guessing at a plausible or persuasive tale that might explain or justify the existence and appearance of the picture. And I mean to argue that this "will to narrate" is not merely a whimsical response to the image, but rather is an inevitable interpretive strategy determined nowadays, firstly, by the popular understanding of the camera as a "time-trap" and, secondly, by the ubiquitous deployment of the still photographic image in contexts that are explicitly narrative, such as newspaper reportage and cinema marketing. Regardless of where a photograph came from originally, regardless of when it was trapped and possessed, it is fertile today only if one can say something about it, literally *about* it—the interpreter must be able to expound or speculate about what went on before and after the photo was taken: one must have an idea of what is a history around and about the spasm of the shutter.

This is to say, the researcher is called upon to work with a fixed image (something which stands as the representation of an instantaneous action) in order to come up with a story— a set of significant actions arranged in duration. As A. Kibedi Varga has written, the puzzle is "how do we get from the action to the story?" Or to ask the question again but differently, "can one suggest a story while only representing an action?"[5] In many cases the puzzle is solved easily. The most common example of the action image which tells a story is probably found in sports journalism. The photo chosen to illustrate the story is often taken from the moment deemed to be "the turning-point," "the game-breaker," the action that caused the result. In this case, the big story is known already, and an aphoristic or representative image can be "animated" in our own minds to represent the flow of the drama before and after the instant of crucial action. The event pictured is a condensation of a series of events whose pattern and outcome are already known.

The rules and the points tables of sporting *fixtures* are just that—fixed, in place, cut and dried. History, even though often written by the winners, is, by contrast, more disputably umpired. Technically the game never finishes, and, accordingly, the whole story is never already known.

Given that very few photographs found in archives are already supplied with stories or interpretations that are agreed upon as "true," one task of the photographic scholar is to "dream up" the history by interpreting clues and cues found in the image and in the context of the overall archive in which the picture has been found. Attempts to establish a "hermeneutics of the photograph" have proven extremely complicated because, although photographs obviously "mean" particular things to particular people (even to particular groups or classes of people), the grammar of such meaning appears lawless and unquantifiable. As Nicholas Peterson wrote in a fine article on popular attitudes to photography: "The way in which people commonly respond to pictures is in any case highly variable: when asked to describe what we see in a picture, we often switch between comments on content, aesthetics, and technique, seeing the picture sometimes from an observer's viewpoint and sometimes from that of its subject."[6]

I believe that this confusion in the laws for interpretation is troublesome only if one holds firm to the idea of history as ineffably true. If one were of a different historiographical persuasion and believed that history is a process of polemics by which narratives currently considered to be true are constantly reviewed by skeptics keen to tell aberrant stories if such new versions can be supported as plausible, then the volatile semiotics of the photograph would be a boon because the picture contains within it the beginnings of so many renegade interpretations. Photographs are often thought to "illustrate" or to "realize" a historical argument as if the past were indeed a sports contest. But to my mind, the real beauty of archival images is that they tend to render the truth of the story more debatable, more fictional. Rather than fixing the truth, the historical photograph usually highlights the dubiety of history.

For example, within a historiographical project that I would wish to support—the accumulation of accusatory tales of white colonial dominion within the South Pacific island territories—a recently discovered collection of photographs can be used as evidence to garnish the reports of exploitation of blacks by whites. But a complicated set of guesses and assumptions is brought into play in order to put the images to work. For these are pictures which seem to testify to a special and laudable relation between colonizer and colonized, between merchant and client, photographer and photographee. These pictures seem to be exceptions that prove a rule.

Thomas Andrew (1855–1939), a New Zealand-born Pakeha, was a professional photographer who set up business in Apia (in the Samoan Islands) in 1891. The extant evidence (or is it merely the evidence that I choose to take notice of?) suggests that most of Andrew's clientele were indigenous Samoans, while his competitors in the region (Messrs. Tatersall and Davis) provided services for the immigrant German and anglophone communities. It seems that a special sense of trust and courtesy was established between Andrew and the Samoans, and this relationship is legible in the images. As the scholars who recently published the pictures explain: "Andrew's photographic 1894–97 portraits of Samoan men and women are explicit documents of their subjects' relation to the photographer. They recorded *Fa 'a Samoa* as pictorial image—a configuration of custom, usage and attitude involving people, god and environment in a union."[7]

When one scrutinizes a selection of Andrew's Samoan pictures in a particular sequence, this account seems the most plausible (as well as most heartening), and I am convinced, on the evidence of *my* reading and viewing of South Pacific history and photography *so far* that this is the "true" interpretation. However, there is no denying, also, that if I altered the sequence of viewing and substituted some "aberrant" Andrew photos for some of the "amiable" ones, then a different interpretation could be supported. For example, if you are presented with the puzzle of interpreting a staring image of a Samoan chief, and if I were to lead up to the presentation of the chief by showing some of the evidently loving and joyous images, it is most likely that the picture would appear to be "about" a dignity or a civility that has germinated in inclement circumstances. Indeed, many such images seem to show the subject's complicity and sophistication in carefully composing his own image for the camera. They show a subject knowledgeably creating his own meaning. However, if the chief is prefaced by two of Andrew's more equivocal and disconcerting Fijian photographs, the image seems to "mean" umbrage or, perhaps, stoicism. The point is that the photograph cannot mean *in itself*: a context, a sequence must be strung around it to support an interpretation. My (not so iconoclastic) assertion is that "truth" or "the real" is not immersed in the image. What can be found in it is an invitation to debate, to maneuver in the cultural politics which *produce* rather than *find* the true.

This definition of truth as communal and negotiable prompts the Australian historian to inquire into the traditions in which photography was located during its inaugural phase in Western societies. If certain interpretive habits can be shown to have persisted from the outset until now, it might be contended that the inaugural beliefs about photography are still in effect and that, moreover, these assumptions are probably now long-standing enough to be thought "natural" or "commonsense."

The most commonly pronounced axiom about early photography is that it was welcomed as a scientific means of rendering the visible world quantifiable. It was contended that a representation of lived experience could now be created with virtually no subjective intervention on the part of an artist. With the prosthetic assistance of mechanized vision, the physical characteristics of life—its scientific blueprint, its underlying truth (different from the debatable, communal truth that I am proposing)— could be trapped, measured, counted, and classified. That is to say, in the orthodox factions of mid-nineteenth-century culture, the more speculative, fictive, or antirealist possibilities for photography were generally ignored in favor of images which confirmed rather than questioned existent worldviews.

The generalist sweep of Jean-François Lyotard's history of bourgeois culture seems germane here. With the development of realist technology, Lyotard argues, the sense of a stable reality was manufactured with overwhelming efficiency:

> The photographic and cinematic processes were able to accomplish better and faster and with a thousand times greater diffusion, much more than pictorial realism and narrative could ever have done, the task that academicism had assigned to realism, i.e. to protect our thinking from doubt. Photography and industrial cinema win hands down over painting and the novel when it is a matter of stabilising the referent, of ordering it from the point of

> view which gives it a recognisable meaning. . . . at the
> same time as it fosters a sense of approval received from
> other people, since all the structures of imagery and se-
> quences really form a code of communication among every-
> one who is sharing in it. In this way, reality effects—or,
> if you prefer, fantasms of realism—are multiplied.[8]

I do not mean to suggest that there was an active conservative conspiracy. It is more plausible simply that photography
was welcomed by institutions which recognized the new "scientific art" as a means of confirming established wisdom rather
than interrogating it or postulating as-yet-unachieved worldviews. Laboratory-style deployment of photography, within
the procedures of scientific inquiry, is obviously part of this
institutional history. But the same corroborative (rather than
speculative) principles applied in the publishing industry,
which was particularly selective in its application of photographs and which "fertilized" the image by "fixing" pictorial
significance within established narrative contexts. As Derrick
Price has contended, the "camera's celebrated 'truth to appear-
ances,' its 'inability to lie' were apparently confirmed precisely
because of the congruence between its images and the literary,
journalistic accounts that preceded it."[9] The photograph was
used to illustrate or confirm the contentions expressed in the
verbal text. Given the connotations of objectivity associated
with photography at the time of its institutional inception,
the canon of existing stories, which ought to have been regarded as *fictional*, or, at least, as constitutive of a negotiable
truth, tended to be perceived as "naturally" true—evidence
could now be presented to support them. Whereas the engrav-
ings and sketches which once illustrated stories in the popular
press were explicitly subjective interpretations, the photograph

(the subjectivity of which was much more implicit) worked to delimit the debatability of the fictions.

The evolution of the nineteenth-century allegory photo exemplifies this drift in "visual rhetoric" from fictional specula-tion through the agency of hand-produced pictures to "truth-ful" confirmation through the evidence of the photograph. In Victorian England the "allegory painting" was a convention developed to store up moral messages about social or religious propriety. Allegory paintings were designed to be catalytic of extant narratives. Like literary allegories they were to be inter-preted not only within the terms of their literal presentation, but also more abstractly within a lore of traditional moral dis-quisition. In this respect the paintings were mnemonic (as were the literary allegories) because they were meant to remind the viewer of the morals that had been taught and stored through a complex of nursery rhymes, biblical tales, and folk and urban legends. The allegory painting or print, which was usually hanging in the family room or the kitchen, was meant to set the remembered stories in play. Most crucially, the painting's meaning (and its "truthfulness") was a function of the "truth-fulness" of its "catalyzed" stories: the painting's meaning could be found only by referring to the world of fiction, a world which is (to state the obvious) *fictional* (but still part of "the real world").

However, when photographers began to create mne-monic images modeled on the allegory paintings, the "truthful-ness" of the morality that was activated in the image seemed to be traceable not only to the fictional world but also to a "natural" domain of experience staged and tested in the light of day. The morals "latent" in the image seemed perceptible in "real" light and "real" time. Narrative was still implicitly involved in the construction of the truth represented by the photograph, but the operations of the storytelling seemed less recognizably fictive now that they were being deployed within a realist regime that was served so well at the time by the scientific apologists of photography. Allegory paintings were explicitly mythic; photographs were only implicitly so. And it is this original "occulting" of the fictive function of the photograph which, even today, makes it difficult to assert that the true fertility of the photographic image is not in its fealty to a material world that shadows ideal truths, but in its potential for calling up stories constitutive of a meaningful but mutable world.

Therefore, the photo becomes historiographically intriguing when it calls up certain established interpretations but also supplies "troublesome" additional information which demands that a new story be created around it. In these circumstances, the archival photo and its historian are working with and against, or on the edges of, what is accepted (so far) as true. One is working with the notorious unruliness of the real world, with the tendency of human systems to be discredited through experience. One is working with and against the canon of historical stories.

In academic terms, this speculative use of the photograph is almost irresponsible, disrespectful as it is of received wisdom. In poetic terms, it is almost an imaginative deployment of imagery which is popularly considered mundane rather than parnassian. In this speculative photo criticism, the image is taken as a symbol and as "an abridgement of nature"[10] from which cultural systems (rather than scientific verities) can be elaborated.

The photo is "fertile," therefore: it is not just a resource for measuring, counting, and comparing. To return briefly to James Agee's understanding of his truth-telling project in collaboration with Walker Evans, exemplary storytellers will use their material to reach beyond the presently quantifiable: "'Description' is a word to suspect. Words cannot embody; they can only describe. But a certain kind of artist, whom we will distinguish from others as a poet rather than a prose writer, despises this fact about words or his medium, and continually brings words as near as he can to an illusion of embodiment."[11] Agee's idea of "embodiment" informs my proposition that the archival photograph is best regarded as "an abridgement of nature," an historiographical resource that is fictive or mnemonic—which is to say, speculative and miniature—as well as quantitative.

The historiographical response to an archival photograph could be construed as a process of remembering and improvising: one recalls all of the credible interpretations of events and motives associated with the concerns of the picture and one attempts to ally those received beliefs with the "aberrant" clues and cues that seem to lurk in the image. Thus the historian interpreting the archival photograph could fairly be described as a purveyor of myth, or as the contemporary counterpart of the singer in folkloric societies as portrayed by Walter Ong:

> the singer is remembering in a curiously public way—remembering not a memorised text, for there is no such thing, nor any verbatim succession of words, but the themes and formulas that he has heard other singers sing. He remembers these always differently, as rhapsodised or stitched together in his own way on this particular occasion for this particular audience.[12]

If the singer is less manifest in society these days as the unifier and purveyor of the stories that define communities, it may not be that the stories have vanished, rather they are being delivered in different forms. In his pithy booklet *Myth and Meaning*,[13] Claude Lévi-Strauss proposes that in eighteenth- and nineteenth-century Europe, once the role of the public storyteller was virtually redundant in industrial/scientific societies, music may have become the principal form by which communities assured themselves that a civil or cultural order prevailed over the chaos of primordial life. Although Lévi-Strauss does not develop the argument, it is tempting to assert that cinema and news reportage have now taken over some of this mythic function in tandem with popular music. Through stories, photographically recorded imagery, and tunes and lyrics, the world—past and present—gets interpreted. Grabs of significance are remembered and "stitched together" with new information repeatedly to form a system of understanding that makes provisional sense, to form histories.

This may seem a rather playful and free-form attitude to historiography. But I do not want to ignore academic protocols of verification. I would not deny that historians have a responsibility to take heed of the current state of truth, mutable as it always is. But I would also like to ensure that we do not undervalue speculative responses to the puzzle of the photograph. Indeed the *uncertainty* which a picture can elicit might be the source of photography's interpretative richness. As E. D. Hirsch argues in *Validity in Interpretation*: "The act of understanding is at first a genial (or a mistaken) guess and there are no methods for making guesses, no rules for generating insights; the methodological activity of interpretation commences when we begin to test and criticise our guesses."[14] Interpretation, then, could be said to arise in a dialectic involving the functions of wit and the discriminations of criticism and comparison. As Paul Ricoeur, who has made use of Hirsch's ideas more than once, explains, "there are no rules for making good guesses,"[15] just as there is no way to teach a poet to invent good metaphors.[16] Because it entails reaching beyond decreed certainty, guessing well cannot be governed by rules. But once the guess is essayed, regulations do apply: "There are methods for validating guesses. This dialectic between guessing and validating constitutes one figure of our dialectic between comprehension and explanation."[17] Ricoeur develops this argument in corroboration of Hirsch: "The procedures by which we test our guesses . . . are closer to a logic of probability than to a logic of empirical verification. To show that an interpretation is more probable in the light of what is known is something other than showing that a conclusion is true."[18]

If interpretation is a dialectical process, therefore, a "true interpretation" might be the ever-modulated product of the interaction between speculation and validation. Whatever gets validated as true then influences what is deemed relevant to future ventures in the quest to establish historical truths. This is how we have objects to guess about: they are deemed worthy to be saved and archived, they are discovered to be potentially significant. Let us persist a little longer with Ricoeur's formulations:

> Could we not say that history is itself the record of human action? History is the quasi-"thing" on which human action leaves a "trace," puts its mark. Hence the possibility of "archives". Before the archives which are intentionally written down by the memorialists, there is the continuous process

of 'recording' human action which is history itself as the sum of 'marks', the fate of which escapes the control of individual actors. Henceforth history may appear as an autonomous entity, as a play with players who do not know the plot. This hypostasis of history may be denounced as a fallacy, but this fallacy is well entrenched in the process by which human action becomes social action when written down in the archives of history. Thanks to this sedimentation in social time, human deeds become 'institutions', in the sense that their meaning no longer coincides with the logical intentions of the actors.[19]

If comprehensible human experience is therefore both *institutive of* and *instituted by* a society's sense of its history, it is logical to conclude that archives are configured according to the patterns of what is already believed. However, if one is prone to skepticism about existent truth, one would also be attracted to the maxim that, with time, a human deed— such as the act of instituting an archive—takes on meanings in excess of the logical intentions of its original perpetrator. And as a skeptical historian, one would aspire to act on that belief to test out which aspects of the received truth can still be corroborated by available information, and which aspects are in need of adjustment.

When the archive in question contains photographs matted with a patina of *time*, the excess of meaning is extreme and one can often do little else than dream up valid stories in response to the images. Such is the task that confronts anyone attempting to tell some truths out of an archive of late nineteenth-century photographs of South Sea Islander canecutters in the Mackay district of Central Queensland.

How to use these images? The first thing is to accept

that they will not tell us anything: rather, we must tell around them. And how do we tell? Through various readings. Firstly, each individual image is scrutinized so minutely that all configurations within the frame are noted and interrelated until a plethora of speculations is tabled. Next, the images alongside it in the archive are cross-referenced one to another, so that the photos (nonspecific as they are in their meanings) construct a polysemous context for themselves. Also, you inquire about the history of the collection: how did it come to exist in this form? Who put it together? How did its systems of classification get established? Then, you read the pictures with reference to other idioms—written reports, statistics, oral histories, gossip, and archaeological evidence. Such reading, in turn, eliminates as implausible certain potential interpretations but also gives rise to new possibilities. Knowing that each idiom has a truth *effect* rather than an inherent truth, you begin to make the guesses and you attempt to validate them. Also, you hope that other skeptical historians will scrutinize the stories to monitor their persuasiveness. Finally you ask yourself: What do I believe now that I have encountered these images? If you are still in business after this question, you start again, with: How can I tell this story best? How can I activate the images and release some of their latent narratives? Then you make your start and you acknowledge constantly the volatility and insufficiency of what you are writing. Or, as Agee put it:

> Let me hope the whole of that landscape we shall essay to travel in is visible and may be known as there all at once: let this be borne in mind, in order that, when we descend among its windings and blockades, into examination of slender particulars, this its wholeness and simulta-

neous living map may not be neglected, however lost the breadth of the country may be in the winding walk of each sentence.[20]

How am I to account for the transfixing quality I find in so many of the Kanaka photos from the minimally catalogued photo collection of the John Oxley Library in Brisbane? If you look for clues in the history of the archive itself, there is little to go on. The photos are stored in drawers classified with the broadest of headings, such as "Kanakas—Sugar ca. 1900," "Kanakas—Mackay—Farleigh Mill, ca. 1890," or "Blackbirding, ca. 1880." Though not absolute, the anonymity of the photos is quite thorough. There are no accompanying written reports from archivists or librarians supplying biographical details about the photographers, their subjects, or the relationships that might have existed between them, although conversations with staff might reveal that many of the images have turned up through repeated public appeals to the citizens and regional libraries of Queensland to send in their old pictures so as to preserve the State's heritage. The John Oxley Kanaka picture collection is thus a standard photographic archive, simultaneously frustrating and enticing in its lack of predetermined, institutional directives for interpretation.

Given that there are so few clues explicit in the structure of the archive itself, you are thrown back on your own responses to the configurations within the frames, allied with trusting to the chance generations of meaning facilitated through the montage of photo to photo within the seemingly random arrangement of the collection—all set against the background of your reading through the myriad histories of Central Queensland and the South Pacific.

"Kanakas." Photographer unknown.
Courtesy of the John Oxley Library,
Brisbane.

"Santo Islander." Photographer
unknown. Courtesy of the John Oxley
Library, Brisbane.

So, how could I explain these three Kanaka photos that I have archived here? Or more accurately, how could I dream up plausible stories to explain why these particular images catch me so piquantly in the context of my reading and viewing in South West Pacific history?

First of all, I acknowledge that the pictures have resonated in my memories of what I judge to be true and urgently communicable in the histories of the Kanakas' involvements in the Queensland sugar industry. Next, I figure how to arrange the pictures and the words about them so that the interpretations are forceful and faithful to my provisional sense of truth. Or, to conscript Agee's philanthropic prose to my task, I must strive to keep faith with ghosts:

> Here at a center is a creature: it would be our business to show how through every instant of every day of every year of his existence alive he is from all sides streamed inward upon, bombarded, pierced, destroyed by that enormous sleeting of all objects forms and ghosts how great how small no matter, which surround and whom his senses take: in as great and perfect and exact particularity as we can name them.[21]

The image of the Santo Islander with the downcast eyes seems endlessly interpretable, but it is imbued with a special hue when placed, firstly, alongside the picture of the couple looking directly at the camera and when read also against the background of an affecting and convincing piece of oral history reportage by Clive Moore.[22] In his article Moore offers a story of Luke Lugomier, a farmer and lay Anglican preacher in the small community of Farleigh just outside of Mackay. Lugomier and his wife, Orrani, both died suddenly of the influenza epidemic which swept through Queensland in late 1919 in the wake of the return of thousands of soldiers who brought the virus back from Europe where the malaise had incubated throughout 1918.

There is a terrible sense of irony in Orrani and Luke's death. Both had lived in Central Queensland for more than thirty years since their separate arrivals in the Mackay district on labor-recruitment boats from the Solomon Islands in the 1880s. They had survived the first wave of epidemic deaths which culled horrific statistics from the indentured laborers. For example, Moore explains that Lugomier arrived from Malaita in September, 1884, when the Islander population in the Mackay district is thought to have been about 3,800; in that same year, 823 Islanders are listed as having died in the region—more than one quarter of the Kanaka population. Moreover, these "deaths were almost totally amongst new recruits."[23] There is a way of interpreting the Lugomier story, therefore, as a tale from the annals of colonialism and immunology: after surviving one viral incursion of the West into South Pacific life, these "model" immigrants succumbed to a rheum brought back, let's say, by a foot soldier son of a pastoralist from Rockhampton who himself survived a battle fought, in another hemisphere, over issues of national expediency, bearing no explicit relation to the South Pacific region.

With such a pall cast about the Lugomier story, we could return to the first two photographs and speculate (somewhat irresponsibly or opportunistically) that the couple depicted so maritally could just possibly be Orrani and Luke, healthy sometime before 1919. I could spin an unverifiable (yet informative) story of contact, or contagion, culture to culture, around this picture of gazes meeting, subject to object, dead-on. Simultaneously, we could wonder about reading grief, or stoicism, or a number of other death-related emotions into the downcast visage of the Santo Islander. Finally, we could scrutinize the trio of statuesque young men standing together in the third photo and we might glimpse death in the image when we notice the blotches and lymphatic swellings on the legs of the men left and right of the image; then we could wonder about advising the John Oxley librarians to estimate the dating of the picture as ca. 1884.

This is to say, in conclusion, that I could make use of the photographs in the context of a skeptical historiography. I could note how the images seemed to crystallize around historical information stored in my memories of reading and viewing around the topics of colonialism, Central Queensland economics, and so on, and I could note how once the stories were called up by the photos, the stories in turn imbued the pictures with particular, perhaps temporary, tones and contrasts, all of them dubious, but all related to the ever-altering store of truth that gets called "history." I could find myself rummaging through the store, finally, to agree again with James Agee about the best wishes and aspirations that one can bring to the writing and reading and seeing of history:

> To come devotedly into the depths of a subject, your respect for it increasing in every step and your whole heart weakening apart with shame upon yourself in dealing with it: To know at length better and better and at length into the bottom of your soul your unworthiness of it: Let me hope in any case that it is something to have begun to learn. Let all this stand however it may: since I cannot make it the image it should be, let it stand as the image it is.[24]

"Kanakas." Photographer unknown.
Courtesy of the John Oxley Library,
Brisbane.

7

Yarning

It takes something like storying to criss-cross the
emptiness. We have formed a taste for the lucky
encounter, for intersection and unrecognised
coincidence, for the story turning round to examine
the storyteller's face.

David Thomson, *Suspects*

In 1953 John Heyer produced, cowrote and directed a
documentary film, *The Back of Beyond*, for the Shell Film Unit
of Australia. For forty years in Europe, Shell had been engaged
in advertising campaigns designed to "naturalize" their products in economies around the industrial world. The general
strategy entailed representing Shell as innate to the good life
available to the citizens of the twentieth century. "You can be
sure of Shell"—the famous slogan is serene and solid, like a
landmass. Emphasizing that Shell was part of Britain's second
nature, the company's public relations exercises often functioned with the assurance and cunning of a myth of origin.
In most cases the PR bespoke the origin of a nation's *modernity*.
Patrick Wright dramatizes the British campaign well:

How does a company strive to control a market when there is no visible difference between its merchandise and that of rival companies? From the twenties onwards—and alongside a whole series of 'secret ingredients' and measures to control outlets—Shell appears to have found a strategy to deal with this problem through advertising. This advertising redefined the countryside in terms of tourism and leisure, and because it did so at a time when so much of the target population was dissociated from traditional relations to the land, it could represent the countryside in strikingly abstract terms. . . . In the more homogenised space of modern communication, distance is no longer experienced in any traditional sense: indeed, Shell restages it as 'the measured mile' with which the motorist causes the countryside to pass in review, as so many miles per gallon. The countryside is a place of strange allure now, a utopian zone which in its 'historical' capacity still holds residues of a former world: traces of an Albion in which time is still cyclical but to which the motorist can still make his progressive way. History, progress, the time of travel all lead to a timeless gestalt of earth with 'nation'. . . .[1]

In Britain, therefore, Shell attempted to conjure a populace of reliable consumers: a populace unified with the beliefs and reactions of a nation served well by its myths of origin; a populace (better known in advertising as a "market") that could remain stable and targetable, like a landmass. Shell strove to conjure a nation of British modernists, for whom petrol-fired technology was innate to the known world. The company aspired to be part of the "natural order" of British contemporaneity.

When, in the fifth year of its existence under the directorship of Heyer, the Shell Film Unit of Australia was given the green light to produce *The Back of Beyond*, similar mythopoeic ends were almost certainly in the minds at the Head Office. However, given the radical displacements of history and geography in which Shell Australia was operating, so far from the Europe of company origins, new or adapted means would be required to evoke the brave, new, modern world of the Branch Office. Indeed, under Heyer's direction the changes were essayed or tolerated, but the adaptations built into *The Back of Beyond* are so *dis*integrative of nationalist sentiment that one is bound to wonder if the film is so determinedly adaptive that it becomes cunningly *mutant* of tried and tested policies.

In prosaic synopsis, *The Back of Beyond* is a documentary about the fortnightly Royal Mail delivery along the Central Australian Birdsville Track, from Maree to Birdsville, and back again. The Mail run kept communication channels open between the outer reaches of the states of South Australia and Queensland, and it thereby fed both a national economy (by maintaining information links between two highly productive primary-industry regions) and a national imaginary (by demonstrating that distance and climatic inclemency could not cleave the bonds of society connecting and galvinizing outpost to outpost). The film rides the Track north from Maree, scrutinizing the ingenuity and stoic good humor of the two mailmen—a laconic Aborigine named Henry and an unflappable Euro-Australian called Tom Kruse. Together they cosset a stripped-down mailtruck (looking indisputably like the prototype for Mad Max's rig in *The Road Warrior*) along the sandblown 300 miles of evanescent Track. They stop at outposts along the way; they sleep rough amidst the natural elements that seem importunately to be working to erase the track from the landscape; they shuttle the truck's payload across the flooded Coopers Creek, to reload onto an even more dilapidated truck on the north bank; and all the while, they chat casually with the incumbents and drifters they encounter, telling and hearing stories as part of their jobs as functionaries of the Royal Mail—conveyors of messages.

Certainly this seems a resumé charged with opportunities to celebrate the cooperation of man and machine and to engender a nationalist pride in a (Shell-sponsored) story of nation-maintenance, of modern culture prevailing over the preternatural. The Shell executive must have thought the film canvased these concerns. A prologue fades up after the Shell logo; in superimposition over an image of desert sands, the text reads:

> The development of inland Australia largely depends on the men who keep open the supply lines and communications—the outback mailmen.
> In an area larger than Europe, beyond the last roads and railways, their tracks make the map of the inland—become the roads of tomorrow—and mark the growth of the Nation.
> This is the story of one of the men and the people he serves—
> THE BACK OF BEYOND

The explicit theme of this introduction is developmentalist, evincing an unequivocal faith in the technology and the aspirations of the modernizing Western nation. In the first live-action sequence of the film, once the "establishing shot" of a centrally spotlighted map of Australia sets the scene, Nature—the old foe and *raison d'etre* of modernization—scowls and swoops in a "primeval" set-piece between an eagle and a rampant frill-necked lizard. The film has started well for the Head Office: Nature, red in beak and claw, awaits civilization. Indeed there is even a note of social Darwinism when the voice-over describes the Track as having its origin in a trade route of "a vanishing race." It is an unpleasant note for the contemporary white liberal; it must be simultaneously tiresome and enraging for the contemporary Aborigine. But for the 1950s developmentalist, it was probably the solipsism required to justify faith in the advance of European technocracy.

In the opening minutes of the film, all the elements—natural and textual—seem in place for a myth of nationalist modernization. The story is set in the "crucible" region of the nation. Douglas Stewart, the literary editor of the perennially jingoistic *Bulletin*, is employed as scriptwriter. Heyer himself is well-credentialed, having been trained in the Commonwealth Film Division under Stanley Hawes, who in turn was a product of John Grierson's grand scheme to produce a proudly chauvinist film unit in every Commonwealth nation.

Moreover, in terms of historical context, a specific "reading light" was already trained on the film. By the 1950s there existed in Australia a well-established genre of developmentalist journalism ready to contextualize and popularize *The Back of Beyond*. Variously named as "landscape writing, travel writing, descriptive writing and several combinations of these labels,"[2] the genre has evolved, especially in the 1930s, as a way "for a great many writers (Ion Idriess, Dora Birtles, Frank Clune, William Hatfield, and Francis Ratcliffe, among those still read today) to foster a broad public debate that was less about "landscape" in any simple or nostalgic sense, than it was about exploring competing scenarios for a future—and usually "high-tech"—Australian society."[3]

With the Shell credit up front, *The Back of Beyond* appeared to be a cinematic cousin of this "futurist" travel-writing. However, it takes very little time for the film to signal its maverick attitudes. Quickly it begins to systematically contradict the Western chauvinism that bleated through the opening voice-

over and credits. Technological progress seems bogged down
in desert sand. The voice-over explains:

> A bare, dry rut disappearing into the mirage, over the edge
> of the world. The Birdsville Track. Where pre-historic ani-
> mals—diprotodon and chronosaurus—dead a million
> years, lie unburied and mingle now their bones with the
> horse, the camel . . . and the white man.

Rather than surging into an evolutionary future, white
civilization seems to have been embraced here by a certain
timelessness. Straight lines—over horizons of new territory,
into the future—take you into mirages of space and time. Circularity is the most reliable motif out here in the terrain that
was initially described to us on the map by the bright ring
of the animator's spotlight, out here where the Mail Run is
an endless repetition—Maree to Birdsville to Maree and back
again—out here where, according to the voice-over, "every
fortnight the story begins." Natural, seasonal time sets a
rhythm, and technological time picks up the beat. This is in
significant contrast to the prioritization of "time-scales" figured in Shell's British campaigns. Patrick Wright explains how
the British scenes usually showed two time-scales operating
symbiotically and profitably and in a master/slave kind of relationship—the eternal returnings of pastoral (seasonal) time
(accompanied by different products for winter and summer
motoring) are comprehended and transcended by *directed* city-
dwellers who can move through the countryside on their way
to the next destination: "The countryside is thus caught up
in a tense movement in which the traditionalist and non-
instrumentalist imagination of 'nature' is displayed against a
stylised celebration of the machine—a movement which asserts
both the cyclical time of the seasons . . . and also the irreversi-

ble historical time of progress, the time which has brought us the motor car."[4]

In *The Back of Beyond*, however, so many of the images and stories are caveats and *memento mori*: the trucks themselves appear mortal even though they are also resolute and brave in the fulfillment of their tasks; townships along the Track lapse into oblivion while others cling to life, like Maree, described as "the ragged flower of a town." The map shows watering holes bearing names such as "The Dead Man." In fact, the film bears witness to only one programmatically developmentalist venture along the Track, namely the government-sponsored dingo-eradication scheme. And given that the scheme is discussed in the context of the scene where Henry and Tom encounter the muttering, knife-wielding "Jack the Dogger"—one of the most dessicated humorists in cinema—all the issues raised around this particular campfire are scorched with Joe's dismissive sense of humor. As Stuart Cunningham notes, this "is about the closest the film comes to a 'line' on development within the terms of national reconstruction."[5]

Once the Company promo has rolled by, therefore, *The Back of Beyond* begins radically to adapt its charter. The film is not a celebration of the triumph of a homogenous technological nation: rather, it becomes a testimonial to a heterogeneous society's humble persistence.

And exactly what kind of society is represented along the Track, where the essence of nationhood is expected to be distilled? Certainly, it is not a community organized according to the traditional hierarchies of English empire. Whereas the vast majority of texts from the travel-genre were "unquestioning of social Darwinist assumptions that Aborigines were naturally doomed to extinction, and that mixed-'race,' even mixed-culture, people incarnated an unholy transgression of the border . . . between nature and culture,"⁶ *The Back of Beyond* manifests no fear or loathing about the possibilities of a motley culture. Produced in an era when Commonwealth Government policy advocated "assimilation" of all "minority races" into a hazy bureaucratic notion of the Anglo-Australian way of life, the film seems remarkably untraumatized by its attraction to the non-Anglo. Indeed it seems positively resistant to the official "homogenizing" policy. It is not interested in minimizing, let alone eliminating, "difference" (defined with reference to an Anglo-Australian norm) in its representations of Track society.

The assimilationist policy is derived from the nineteenth-century European positivism which gave rise to nationalism and to the rhetorics of modernization and modernism. It is a "social fitness" mentality that found its Australian expression most stridently in the years leading up to the enactment of Federation on the first day of the twentieth century. William Lane's incandescent prose epitomizes the developmentalist faith, out of which assimilationist policies, Commonwealth Government Film Divisions, and technophiliac advertising campaigns could spring:

> We are for this Australia, for the nationality that is creeping to the verge of being, for the progressive people that is just plucking aside the curtain that veils its fate. Behind us lies the Past with its crashing Empires, its falling thrones, its dotard races; before us lies the Future into which Australia is plunging, this Australia of ours that burns with the feverish energy of youth, and that is wise with the wisdom for which ten thousand generations have suffered and toiled.⁷

However, an alternative tradition has persisted from the same Federation era, a tradition that helps us understand and locate *The Back of Beyond*. The shining exemplar in this case might be Joseph Furphy's *Such Is Life* (1903). The novel is a complex meditation on narrative, democracy, social memory, and political change. Set in the Riverina district on the border between New South Wales and Victoria, the text is an elaborate polyphony of stories relayed, one to another (and thereby also to the reader), by an array of characters many of whom reinvent themselves several times throughout the novel. (One is reminded of the voice-over in *The Back of Beyond* which describes Birdsville as a place "where a man can ride down the main street out into the hills and perish, or turn up on the coast with a new name." One is put in mind also of Max's chameleon qualities in *Mad Max: Beyond Thunderdome*.) It is an "Australian" novel, but one which constantly demands a reconceptualization of "Australia." As Ivor Indyk has noticed:

> Instead of a sense of national identity, there is a constant assertion of national differences. The characters are English first or Irish, Scottish, Cornish, Chinese, Dutch, German, French or Aboriginal—with each group having its own distinguishing dialect. Even where two bullockies belong to the same group, it will nevertheless make a great deal of difference if one of them comes from Victoria, the other from New South Wales.[8]

In Furphy's comprehension of Australia there is no sense of racial destiny, no executive caste, no mainstream into which all subsidiary influences will dissolve. Rather Furphy's nation is a concert of interrelated yet autonomous entities. The novel's form embodies the society it seeks to anatomize. Or, as Miles Franklin and Kate Baker wrote in their canny study of Furphy, the novel has "a design as skillfully reticulated as those of the stockwhips of Riverina Proper—works of craftsmanship and durability made of kangaroo hide, each strand of which can be traced as it disappears and reappears throughout its length."[9]

The Back of Beyond also bears comparison to the Riverina stockwhip. The film assembles a cast of yarning wanderers crisscrossing the line of the Track. Motifs appear, disappear, and then reappear at unexpected moments, as with the dingoes and snakes that insinuate the narrative. An array of separate yet contiguous cultural representatives function symbiotically to form the *gestalt* of Track society: the camel-trader Bejah with his Islamic code; Henry with his relaxed stoicism and catholic taste in gramophone jazz; the Aboriginal stockman named Malcolm Arkarinka who hitches a ride with Henry and Tom to return to his "own country" which is later shown to be the ruins of the creole Lutheran-Aboriginal pastoral monastery where he was raised; the self-effacing Euro-Australian Tom with his easy conversational facility with all factions; Old Joe the Rainmaker scrutinizing the sky in a cosmic call and response routine; the chorus of voices on the shortwave radio network calling and responding to the heavens according to a different set of protocols. If the film has strength and resilience, it is because of the tangle of discrete elements that comprise it.

The film can be understood in terms of the stockwhip, therefore. Or, to mutate Franklin and Baker's metaphor, *The Back of Beyond* is more like the runs of succulent creeper vines that are planted along Australian beachfronts to hold sand in place against erosion—the sand supports the vine and all its robust tributary tendrils running axially off the main stem, and because of this support the tendrils proliferate and flourish to the extent that, firstly, *they* must also be understood as mainstream, and that, secondly, they cause the sand to remain as nutrient matrix. The creepers are nature deployed as culture, and vice versa, to the extent that the distinction between the two terms is tenuous. Analogously, the Track society is the sum of its interconnecting yet autonomous people, stories, and geographies; the society exists amidst the natural elements *because* the Track is there, and the people and their stories *cause* the Track to prevail.

Bearing in mind that *The Back of Beyond* is a Shell product, made by a crew of technologist Anglo-Australian men during the assimilationist 1950s, it is tempered with a remarkable narrative *humility*. As noted already, the "drive" of the film's plotting is marked by a systematic disavowal of customary (Western) narrative progress straight through "frontiers" of ignorance and enigma. In *The Back of Beyond* straight lines lead into mirage. Motifs of *circularity* abound: the gramophone provides emotional commentary for the narrative's restlessness; the importunate wheels of the truck repeatedly attract Ross Wood's inventive cinematography; the truck itself accelerates in a huge arc as it builds up speed in order to breach the sandhills; the punt swings into a rotating drift when it spins out of human control (into its "natural" pattern of movement) when Tom falls overboard during the Coopers Creek crossing sequence (which itself is an interlude of patient, recurrent departures and returns); there is also the meticulous rhythm of dialogue and mediation that is required to send messages on the radio, especially in the scene on the banks of the Cooper when Tom acts as go-between to facilitate a discussion between the flying doctor and an ailing patient whose signal, like her vitality, has become too weak to reach the medic direct.

All these tropes "mean" something resolutely different from the "paranoid driving force"[10] or through-line that usually motivates technological travel-narratives. Instead of pitching the mind to the destination, where the frontier of ignorance or wildness will have been pushed away by the achievements of culture, the film functions interpretively through "an arc of reconsiderations."[11] This is to say, that at crucial stages through the narrative, the audience can orientate themselves most effectively by reassessing information that was not "efficiently" processed and controlled earlier. For example, the status of the dingo is a running enigma in the film. At first it is figured as a proud predator, glimpsed in Landseer framing from beside the road. Later it is redefined by Jack the Dogger, who preys on the predator and can find no heroics in the scenario. This interlude in turn reverberates with a foregoing scene in which Tom and Henry are stalked by edge-of-frame snakes and dingoes while the men are digging the truck out of a sandbog: in adroit suspense-cutting the men chatter on seemingly oblivious while the narrative pressure of threat builds up—the conventions of through-line plotting set up an immediate future of jeopardy which then must be revised a few moments later when Henry and Tom, casually, free the wheels and set out again, unimpeded. Furthermore, the sandbog scene is retrospectively adjusted *again* in the scene with Jack the Dogger when Tom reveals that he had seen the dingo earlier and that, implicitly, for *him*, the sandbog scene was already different from the suspense scene which the audience thought they were witnessing.

The arcs of reconsideration generate a degree of humility in the audience. As we negotiate the course of the narrative we get used to the idea that we are fallible and in need of constant reeducation: "Every fortnight, the story begins." And at countless moments during each fortnight, the story mutates against our expectations. Take, for example, the introduction to the Mission scene. The truck, with Henry, Malcolm, and

Tom aboard, approaches the ruins of Father Herman Heinrich Vogelsang's Utopia late at night. The voice-over talks reassuringly of the old community as a haven even in decay. It is a "sanctuary for the traveler who likes to sleep where man has put his hand." No sooner does this paean to the pioneers of Culture conclude than, in extreme foreground, a huge knife is jagged down from out of frame to come to rest, glinting moonlit, in a deadwood log. This is Jack the Dogger's entry into the narrative, and the pastoral tone has been quickly negated. The voice-over requires reconsideration; the underside of every narrative development must be heeded; the unexpected, the out-of-frame must all be acknowledged as "present." The scene continues with the same mutative impetus when Malcolm wanders through the chapel ruins. "This was to be our Promised Land," he muses elegiacally as he recalls his bizarre creole dreaming, which entails memories of pastoral fecundity, sedentary farming culture, and Aboriginal-dialect liturgies of Latin-derived Lutheran benedictions (yet another call-and-response sequence knitting meaning and memory into the Track society). But while Malcolm recounts the vision splendid to his mind's eye, the camera eye registers a routed scene. Everything he remembers is now in decay. There is no evidence to corroborate his vision splendid.

The peculiarities of Track culture are not to be taken for granted. The past and present of the region cannot be comprehended through the interpretive frame of presumption. Whereas a conventional colonial-English narrative would select and fit information to the pattern of triumphal (riddle-solving, impediment-eradicating) storytelling about the arrival and establishment of Track society, *The Back of Beyond* tends to deny the validity of an Anglican system of heroics or a prioritization of white culture as the standard into which difference will be assimilated. Characters such as Bejah, Joe the Rainmaker, and Malcolm and Henry are so thoroughly "present" that they cannot be expected to dissolve in the homogenization of Government Policy. In Stuart Cunningham's terms, "these figures occupy spaces outside of, but at the same time before and beyond the temporal boundaries of white settlement, and from which white settlement must graft its instincts for survival."[12] As that rather rare ethnographic document, a Western interpretive system which tacitly acknowledges that it is operating in a foreign territory, the film finds ways to show its uncertainties and its readiness to adapt. It is in this respect that there is a degree of humility functional in the narrative.

Ross Wood's precise camerawork enhances the sense of mutability, reconsideration, reeducation, and humility. The film is formally "restless" rather than "assertive." It evokes the thematic issues of uncertainty and reconsideration, but it never looks uncertain, confused, or unresolved. In visual terms, the film "thinks" lucidly about contradiction and reappraisal. The space figured through the *mise en scene* is almost boundless in its depth. From the extreme foreground to the horizon, all perceptible space is crisply in focus and is, therefore, replete with visual meaning. Everywhere the camera looks, something of limpid visual significance is likely to occur. Jack the Dogger's foregrounded knife is one example. The shot which introduces Bejah is another: the camera is trained downward on Tom working underneath the truck; Tom climbs out and stands up in extreme close-up, foreground; he turns and walks away from camera, toward the midground, calling out to Bejah who is in the extreme background; Bejah ambles right to left across frame and veers toward a destination off-camera; the camera pans away from Tom and dwells on Bejah as he moves out

of background, through midground into foreground on his
way to his prayer-mat on top of a ridge overlooking the desert.
At no stage during this complex and fluid shot is focus adjusted. Everything that is framed looks razor-sharp; every portion in the picture and every area that can be panned to is
clearly significant. The world of meaning is everywhere and
it outreaches our customary focusing abilities and interpretive
frames: pan left and there is more crystalline information to
consider, more information by which to adjust what we have
learned so far. Start a shot on a man tinkering in the shade
of a truck and finish on another man contemplating the Koran
in white desert light. The film finds formal means to show
that such outlandish connections should be expected as normal
in the social and semiotic space being represented.

The sandbog sequence is also organized around this
principle of the expansiveness of the world of meaning. The
road-determined, mail-scheduled *line* of narrative is knocked
out of shape both by the stories (from other places, other
times) that Henry and Tom tell each other while they dig under
the surface of the road, and by the outside story-elements
(snakes, dingoes, owls) that approach the road transverse to
the functional delineation of the Track. The microcosm of Tom
and Henry is assailed by influences on the edges of its confines.
Then, in the shot to end this dramatic interlude, the scenario
is recontextualized in a huge wide shot which shows the
sandbog drama to be a tiny, albeit *clearly significant*, incident
in a larger, virtually boundless environment.

This procedure of emphatically adjusting the shot-scale
is recurrent throughout the film and it is part of a systematic
process of scenographic "de-dramatization."[13] The film repeatedly reminds the viewers of the modesty of scale that humanity
assumes along the Track. The human presence in the environ-

ment is repeatedly "put in its place." This is not to say the people are discounted—society is shown to prevail along the Track, even if the prevalence is always only provisional—but there are practically no heroics associated with the persistence. The de-dramatization is well exemplified in the interlude on the bank of the Cooper, when Tom operates the radio to relay life-and-death information from Mrs. Mac to the flying doctor, across hundreds of uninhabited miles, while Henry and Malcolm lounge on armchairs, eating beefsteak, in a makeshift open-air sitting-room festooned with flotsam and bric-a-brac deposited by the Cooper's floodwaters. In a surreal realignment of the dramatic/spatial dynamics of domestic melodrama, an "intimate" sick-bed scene is played out in the most banal manner possible—Tom brushing flies away as he drones the call signs over and over before relaying each detail of symptom; Malcolm and Henry pragmatically continuing to consume their meals. The inchoate melodrama is attenuated across a "theoretical" media space which separates the protagonists from one another and precludes the possibilities of a drama based on the traditional scenography associating emotional intensity with physical proximity.

Indeed the heroic or dramatic potentialities of *distance* as a narrative element are constantly downplayed as part of the programmatic de-dramatization. Tom, the man who vocationally negotiates fortnightly tracts the size of European nations, is systematically portrayed as nothing more than a "character," *not* a *hero*, in this film full of "characters." As Stuart Cunningham has observed, the film is organized by a "tentative defiance" of the codes of heroization that typified the British documentary treatment of films concerning work and communications. Even though Tom is centered as the protagonist (as the *driver*, in fact), "distractions" are methodically provided by the incidental characters—Malcolm, Bejah, Jack, Mrs. Oldfield of Etadinna conversing on the station radio—who occupy narrative centrality at different stages through the trek. Furthermore, Tom is repeatedly "destabilized" as orienter and activator of the narrative. For example, there are the enigmas about his home life. Is the woman who calls him to dinner in Maree his wife? What is in the private letter which the Maree postman was so keen to give Tom and which Tom was uninterested in accepting once he had become a nomad again and which Tom was about to peruse (with the camera lurking over his shoulder) when the nondrama of Mrs. Mac's salvation occurred? Indeed, note how little is made of the inherent "heroics" of the Mrs. Mac scenario. "This won't buy the baby a new dress," chirps Tom as he hangs up the radio mouthpiece before dusting himself off and cajoling Malcolm into taking another load across the Cooper. With regard to Tom as a narrative function, a viewer accustomed to the premises and procedures of John Grierson's proletariat heroics or Pare Lorenz's metaphysics of labor and development, "would expect more neatness in a documentary . . . intent on providing a stable, knowable characterisation as a spectator's entrée into its world."[14]

Considering the "Outback-narrative" orthodoxies already in existence in 1953, Heyer and Stewart chose to commandeer and adapt the least heroic tradition. They chose to dramatize (or de-dramatize) the most minimalist of attitudes. It can be argued that the ground rules of "Outback-narrative" were laid in a few originary texts from the 1830s and 1840s, namely the exploration journals of the "triumphalist" Thomas Mitchell, on the one hand, and the more "humble" and adaptive testimonials of Charles Sturt and Edward Eyre on the other.[15] (The arrogance of William Lane and the sardonic self-deprecation of Joseph Furphy might be understood to have developed respectively within the two historical attitudes personified early by Mitchell and Sturt or Eyre.) As he characterizes himself in his journals, Mitchell deals with distance and terrains vitalistically. Space is portrayed as a challenge, a theatre of operations in which achievements—arrival, possession, survey, cultivation—are the inevitable and indelible results of an energetic (and mechanically "advantaged") Englishman's dominion over "pristine" tracts of land. He is fortified by a *droit du seigneur* which will not be thwarted. Sturt and Eyre, by contrast, describe chastening ordeals in the landscape and they interpret the experiences as sentimental educations. They come to comprehend distance and the natural elements as factors to be persevered, heeded, and acknowledged with respect and humility. They learn to overcome the *hubris* that impels a traveler to traverse a territory quickly, to subdue it to the dictates of a predetermined schedule. They take their lessons from the text of the country (most importantly also they both learn from the Aborigines who offer advice and "interpretations" along the way); they move when the elements say "go now." They learn to travel light and to follow the line of least resistance, to adapt to the dictates of the country. Moreover they have learned that the environment which they inhabit and alter (at the same time as it alters them) is constantly *in process*: nothing is "naturally" permanent, especially culture. In Sturt and Eyre's texts there is a preparedness to admit that, firstly, the English myths which impelled them into the country do not withstand a lengthy test of experience, and that, secondly, no story which is sustainable has an enduring effect unless you are willing to recommence at every conclusion. "Every fortnight the story begins."

In *The Back of Beyond* Tom, Henry, Malcolm, and Bejah

are never assertive dominators of their environment. They do not acculturate. They improvise and cooperate. Whatever the waters of the Cooper dictate, Henry and Tom do it. If a sandstorm blows in, the wind saying "go now," they break camp and move on. They weigh the options, always acknowledging that for every call to action there is never just one way, never only one direct line regulating Australian nature into Western culture. "Which way are you going now, over the sandhill or across the creek?" asks Henry early in the film, thereby signaling as thematic the idea of the multiplicity of options all the way along the Track.

There is rarely only one way. And a new way need not be *entirely* new. Old and new, autocthanous and imported, commingle throughout the film. Malcolm's complicated Lutheran Dreaming with its local-dialect/Latinate liturgy is one deliberately controversial example of Heyer's passion for adaptation and hybridization. More light-hearted is the sagely self-mocking story Henry tells about his attempts to improvise a gear wheel out of coolibah wood. As Henry happily admits, the bush remedy did not work at all in that instance, but the thrill and the necessity of habitually essaying such ingenuity are emphasized rather than ridiculed by the pragmatic humor of Henry's final observation: "Good wood, coolibah . . . you can make a lot of things. . . ." Or, to move from the particular to the general, the film itself can be interpreted as Heyer's deliberate and quite perverse adaptation of that model GPO Film Unit product, *Night Mail*. The celebrated poet con-scripted to write the commentary, the mail-and-communi-cations theme, the dramatic emphasis on the vehicles that carry the messages (literally and thematically), the narrative pat-terned to the deadline of a "time-tabled" journey: Grierson's and Heyer's films share crucial motifs and concerns. But *Night*

Mail seems deliberately to have been melted and remolded almost beyond recognition in the white light of the Track.

Indeed, the script repeatedly states how the Track environment sets conditions in which the solid, the actual, the pre-
sumably "real" can be transmogrified according to the dictates
of imagination. The Track is "a bare dry rut, disappearing into
the mirage, over the edge of the world." If travelers were to
pause and scan the horizon, they would see how they occupied
an "empire of bare stone" (a slate continually wiped clean,
perhaps—not a *terra nullius*, but a surface inviting repeated
and ever-different inscriptions). They would notice also how
they were "shut in by a wall of mirage." As exemplified by
the Bunuelesque scene showing the open-air sitting-room on
the banks of the Cooper (in which Henry's selection of jazz
syncopates the "timelessness" of the environment), the film repeatedly presents landscapes which are "both real and surreal,
denotative and connotative."[16] This is an environment which
requires a penetrating percipience, an ability to see and think
past the obvious. If the Track inhabitants are to survive, they
must be able to envisage the enlivening mirages of the not-yet-
existent as well as to discern the invidious mirages of folly
and impracticality.

The landscape rendered by the film is animated by "unconscious" energies and entities that are perhaps surreal, perhaps simply ancillary to the more explicit, superficial properties
of the Track. The yarns that characters spin to each other, the
legends that "rise up" along (and *across*) the Track—the reanimation of Father Vogelsang's presence in Malcolm's memory,
the tale of the lost girls who "vanished under windblown
sand"—all these ancillary narratives are emphatically present
even if they are latent. Similarly, to travel along the Track is
to play a keyboard of myth which makes the mind chime with

the names of settlements now erased from the surface: "Miramitta, Appatumpna, Kuralpininna, Ooroowoolanni . . . Ooroowoolanni . . . The people are gone. Their stories live on in the legends and tales of the Track, travelling as they did across the sand and stones."

An animism galvanizes the landscape (and the film, therefore), but it has very little to do with mysticism or the transcendence of the mundane. In the same decade as Heyer and Stewart arrived at their "humble" narrative attitude, Patrick White's novel *Voss* (1957) would also explore the futility of the European drive to *defeat* the continent. However, White's novel still allows the traditional European-heroic attitude to survive in the, admittedly, rarefied realm of metaphysics. In White's novel, Voss's arrogance causes his physical death, but it also allows his apotheosis. Stewart and Heyer, on the other hand, remain pragmatic and secular in their dramatization of persistence rather than martyrdom in the Outback. *Voss* has been repeatedly and correctly judged to have been ahead of its time in the white Australian cultural context. It seems to me that *The Back of Beyond* with its refusal to take solace in a spiritual alibi, is even more "avant garde" inasmuch as it examines the questions of how to live, here and now, with an adapted mentality. *Voss*, by contrast, evades answering the pressing secular questions even as it urgently raises them. By comparison, the legends called up by *The Back of Beyond* are utterly pragmatic, cautionary tales to be heeded and applied in the secular world. The ghosts of the Track are part of daily life, if life is to prevail. The tale of the lost girls is a lesson about the laws of Outback life: the children were not taught how to use the radio, and therefore they perished; Father Vogelsang's Mission is animated with the chastening testimony of Ozymandias—"all gone now . . . all gone now." A society must first survive as a secular entity before its spirit can burgeon. The film is galvanized by a *secular* animism, therefore.

Toward the end of *The Back of Beyond* there is a moment which reveals where much of Heyer's advice for survival might be coming from. After the tale of the lost girls is finished, the truck arrives in Birdsville, and the film wanders around the township observing vignettes, pausing to record a scene where an Aboriginal woman is seated in a circle with a multi-racial gang of children. The woman speaks to the children and makes handprints in the sand; the children copy the prints. The commentary gives its interpretation of the scene: "The remnants of native lore are passed on from black to white, and children learn to read the ancient book of the sand, a game that may mean life or death." The woman is passing on her share of the huge and complex corpus of knowledge that makes up Aboriginal law for the district; she is participating in a system of narrative cooperation which ensures that the security of a society is shared and guaranteed by the entire society rather than by an executive class or individual. Eric Michaels explains the law-maintenance system (or *Jukurrpa*) as he understands its operation in Warlpiri society:

> This Law, in its characteristic story forms, is distributed differentially across the population. Age, gender, kinship category and 'country' determine who might access which aspects of the knowledge, which parts of songs, what designs or dance steps. . . . [Social] accounting (ceremony, storytelling, decision-making) requires assemblages of kin to constitute the Law. Stories reach 'over the hill' to the next community and to the next person. A long story, a full myth, a major decision, requires many people, enmeshes many communities, in its enactment.[17]

This is a description of a society which survives on its storytelling, or, more technically, it survives on the *delegation*[18] of its storytelling. It is a society with enough humility to acknowledge that the world of meaning and of responsibility to one's environment is larger than the capacity of any one person or information-storage system. It is a society that functions primarily on *interaction* rather than coercion or dominion. And I would contend that it is a society that is the blueprint for the community that is "making a go of it" along the Track in Heyer's version of the polyglot Outback. In the final analysis, *The Back of Beyond* is a celebration of the efficacy of yarning: Tom carries the written messages of the Royal Mail, but he also stops off to talk about how much feed is left in the lower reaches of station properties; Henry tells about accidents and ingenuity; the cast of women who perform outstanding cameo roles along the Track interweave the airwaves with their radio conversations; Joe the Rainmaker resolutely maintains his rituals (and the Cooper *has* recently been replete); Bejah holds his life in place with the incantations from the Koran. They all call each other into a society that survives through the assiduous communication of a myriad polyglot calls and responses.

The Back of Beyond knits it all together as it knits itself together.

8

Yondering

A Reading of MAD MAX Beyond Thunderdome

"WELCOME! OPEN YOUR BOOK AT PAGE ONE."
In the final stages of *MAD MAX Beyond Thunderdome* this message rings out from a gramophone disc, a record of the past, which the lost tribe of children have been carrying with them in their exile. To the characters within the narrative, and to the viewers outside of it listening in, the declamation resounds with an oracular tone. At least two riddles are thereby posed.

In the case of the children, they have always deduced, from scant information condensed in their fogged memories, that the disc is some kind of sonic generator, and they have been using it (albeit doubtfully) in a way that is spiritually effective even though no material benefits have been manifest. However, it is not until Max has operated a turntable and stylus for them that they comprehend how the record once fitted into another system that created specific meanings. Availed of their new knowledge, the children see that they have been mis-applying their found artifact. Or more precisely, they have been applying it for a different purpose, in a different significative system.

So, with Max manipulating the circulation of the record, the motley tribe hearkens to the oracle. Appropriately enough, these infantile practitioners of a mutated Austral-English are listening to the first installment of a self-tutorial foreign lan-guage program for English speakers. The gramophone disc poses a conundrum, therefore: in a polyglot community, how might one negotiate the trade of truth and belief from one culture to another?

This leads directly to the second riddle: how can one confidently assess the exact tonal register of this film? What is its voice, what is its "attitude," and ultimately what might it be "about?"

In answer to both riddles, the gramophone is emphatic: "Open your book at page one." The voice is a *deus ex machina*, and it is calling for a start; it is alerting the characters and the audience to the notion of *origins*. And here the film signals that it is unequivocally mythological. That is to say that *Mad Max 3* conclusively adopts an enunciative register that had been invoked only intermittently in the earlier films.

The first *Mad Max* is predominantly naturalistic in its art direction, its time setting ("a few years from now") and its characterization. Even its horror is expressed in a suburban, or *worldly*, idiom of verbal crudity, mechanical cacophony, and automotive and editorial speed. Of course, the film has a flavor of fantasy, but it has an even stronger whiff of plausibility. It is notable that George Miller has spoken repeatedly of his original conception of the film as a report on the road carnage endemic to Australian society. Despite all its genre cues and its fetishism of automobilia, *Mad Max 1* remains representational rather than, say, surrealist or escapist. The roads are recognizable and, although they lead to the badlands, they are badlands that one can get to on a Sunday drive.

The second *Mad Max (The Road Warrior)* is far less tied to the everyday. This is not to say that it is patently concerned with examining or purveying myth, even though the legendary status of Max is emphasized in the homeric prologue and even though close attention is paid in scripting to reworking the topos of the wanderer's trek through a purgatorial wasteland. Rather, because the suspense cinema devices of subjective camera-placement, movement, framing, and cutting are honed so keenly that the mechanics of the narrative are themselves a source of wonder (the editing is better tuned than any pursuit vehicle), the filmmakers build a hot rod of a film that could best be interpreted as principally formalist or stylistic. For example, the celebrated appearance of Wez suddenly from under the bonnet of the beleaguered rig near the end of The Chase is so effective and in keeping with the spirit of the entire film not only because the frame-invasion trick is reliably startling, but also because the audience acknowledges, somewhat sardonically, that it is *that device again!*

Kennedy-Miller have never underestimated the cinematic literacy of the contemporary audience, and they have repeatedly reaped the benefits of relying on this collective savvy. There is a sense all through *Mad Max 2* that, if the film deals with anything that must be counted as "real," then it is fundamentally about storytelling and the cinema rather than any habitable world which the film might represent, reflect, or impinge upon. The second film of the trilogy simply has too

few of the ploys and conventions of naturalism for a sociological or realist critique of it to be of much value.

Of course, *MAD MAX Beyond Thunderdome* is also centrally concerned with storytelling. Its bardic sense is made no
less significant by the comic verve accompanying it. The popular, *participatory* aspects of mass entertainment are being celebrated. If a film can be regarded and heard as an orator, then
the institution of cinema is quite properly a sophisticated oral
science—all the orators from all the film industries around the
globe can be said to *communicate* to form a huge, unquantifiable mythology. Thus, when the ringmaster of the
Thunderdome turns to the camera to confide the artifice of
it all, he need have no doubt that sooner or later everyone
will know that Max's story can make sense only if viewers are
able to recognize the reenactments and the rhetorics from a
myriad cinematic stories. For example, without beginning to
strain credence, one can cite deliberate quotes in *Beyond
Thunderdome* from *North by Northwest, Casablanca,* the
"Roman" films of fifties Hollywood, *Apocalypse Now, The Shining,* and Sergio Leone's westerns. Every sight and sound in
Beyond Thunderdome is part of a folk history. Every sight and
sound is carrying vestigial messages from the repeated ceremonies of cinema-going, and the film knows this, the film is about
this liturgy, and it tells its watchers so.

However, episode three of Max's saga takes on an added
dimension (dare I say a certain grandeur?) because the urge
to *narrate* is shown to be a central theme of the film. *Beyond
Thunderdome* declares itself incontrovertibly to be mythic. It
demands to be interpreted that way. What's more, it is designed as a *primary* myth: a myth of origins, a type of Genesis.
The film and its characters are destined to tell stories not just
obliquely about the cinema, but also quite explicitly about col-

onization, ethical realignment and social gestation. Whereas the moral scheme organizing *Mad Max 2* is no more perspicuous or evangelical than the virtues underscoring the aestheticised anarchy of Merry Melodies cartoons, the precepts of *Beyond Thunderdome* loom enormous because the film is dealing in primary myth, in a narrative system that prescribes the histories of a community.

The film repeatedly declares itself to be generically Australian (which is to say it is also generically transgeneric). In the first ninety seconds, the insignia of nationality abound. Kennedy-Miller's trademark is first up—the "BHP of the culture-industry" proudly present themselves along with their newest product. Then almost immediately, the initial image hazes up: of course it is The Desert. Next, we get Bruce Spence and Mel Gibson, the former whooping his caricatural, antipodean head off, the latter squinting from his desirable corporate-Australian visage. Clearly, the film is to be a festival of leitmotifs and icons from white Australian cultural history. Quite apart from Frank Thring, there are . . . the convict escaping from his penal hell, the prophet emerging purified from the desert, the lost children from numberless bush legends all sheltering in a fecund haven concealed in the blasted interior. These are all cliches, admittedly, but the sophistication of *Beyond Thunderdome* is that it analyzes and redeploys the cliches, knowing them to be usefully true because the community recognizes them as truisms. It knows that two or three cliches can be an embarrassment; but hundreds of them constitute a mythology which can embody the many complexities of history and aspiration contested by a national community.

For example, the welter of cliches in *Beyond Thunderdome* conjoin to evoke a sophisticated antipodean cosmology of inversion and redemption, wherein a saintly seer might logically (and meaningfully) be dressed in black and blinded by a comic mask as he rides backwards toward the future and toward, perhaps, yet another beginning now that the features of his identity have been obscured. This one composite image, cobbled from a few commonplaces of legend, constitutes a condensed and evocative metonym of many tomes of white Australian history. In short this film is dealing in vibrant contemporary myths, myths of colonial canniness.

Beyond Thunderdome is one tale from this collection of stories of origin. One might call such a collection a mythology, or one might prefer to call it a history. As in most modern colonial societies the difference is harder to discern the closer one looks for it. Certainly, Australian historiography takes its shape from the myths of creation which colonists enacted while establishing the European society in an ostensibly empty locale. Mark Twain's famous comment that "Australian history is almost always picturesque . . . [that] it does not read like history but like the most beautiful lies,"[1] makes sense with reference to this process of prefiguring actuality by fiction. It is a certain type of fiction, a structuring fiction, a myth of origins, that gets enacted in the antipodes. As Twain extrapolated about the lies, "they are all true, they all happened."

Thus, when the children in *Beyond Thunderdome* repeat their stories of arrival, settlement, and destiny, when they fashion an adaptive language comprised of words, sound effects, gestures, and the parting curtains and focusing frame of cinema, all in order to make sense of their present predicament, and when Max himself begins to learn this language and these stories, the audience is privy to some beautiful lying. Commensurately, earlier in the film, in another arena of origin, Aunty Entity (Tina Turner's character) describes Bartertown: "Where there once was a desert, now there's a town; where there was despair, now there's hope; where there was robbery, now there's trade." It amounts to one bright word: "Civilization!"

Her colonial admiration of order echoes countless tracts from the annals of white Australia. Take for example David Collins's rendition of the first English encampment at Port Jackson: "[The] spot which had so lately been the abode of silence and tranquillity now was changed to that of noise, clamour and confusion: but after a time order gradually prevailed everywhere. As the woods were opened and the ground cleared, the various encampments were extended, and all wore the appearance of regularity."[2]

If a society and its habitat have a shape, it is an arbitrary one which can be scrutinized and renovated as the communities demand. It is the shape of history, which is in turn the shape of the myths of origin. With reference to the social milieux pictured in *Beyond Thunderdome*, Bartertown is shaped to a particularly crude and brutal myth of commerce, while the Crack in the Earth is regulated by fairytales of excessive innocence, and Max's wastelands bear up under connotations of purgatorial trial and renaissance. The landscape of *Beyond Thunderdome* is kept barely safe from erosion by these little plots of culture.

All this determinedly local historiography would be of little consequence had the legend of Mad Max not been taken as universally relevant, and, perhaps, even universally true, during the 1980s. Through an accident of world history, entailing developments such as the telecommunications revolution, international monetary upheavals, the "emergence" of a politically assertive Third World, the imminence of the *fin de siècle*, and the continuing ransom of Armageddon, the world seems presently to require myths of origin and recommencement. And the tales of white Australia, stamped as they are with an impression of historical veracity, supply shapes for such myths. (Herein could lie one explanation for Australia's high stakes in the current international cultural market.)

In this context of a contemporary vogue for stories of renaissance, one can see that the style of *Beyond Thunderdome* is well suited to its themes. Clearly the film is stitched together from innumerable fragments and quotes, be they cinematic, literary, or even painterly. For example, it seems appropriate that some of the savage children should resemble so closely John White's sixteenth-century portraits of American Indians, while others look like slightly addled versions of the Care Bears. Clearly, the film invites descriptions of its "post-modernity."

Now, I happen to think the *Beyond Thunderdome* is too resonant to be summarized adequately by any one critical term, and should I employ labels from time to time throughout this essay, I must emphasize straightaway that the epithets are meant to be facilitative rather than conclusive of our thinking. This said, I would like to assay the film's postmodernism for a few paragraphs.

Beyond Thunderdome confirms Max as a "hero-despite-himself," or as a hero suffused with a sense of ambiguity, a hero celebrated anthemically by the song "We Don't Need Another Hero." The project announced by Fifi in *Mad Max 1*—to give the people back their heroes—is fulfilled, but with an ironic camber because Max has still not learned to be either consistently or voluntarily altruistic. One of the special characteristics of the film is this tendency for definitions inherited from the past to alter or mutate even as they are being applied. This volatility is appropriate to the tale of a culture that is "beginning (again) at page one." In such a circumstance, all available signs and artifacts might be counted temporarily equal, or even interchangeable. In such a circumstance, there would be no certainty, for example, that the hero who might be constituted at the *end* of page one would be the same entity you started with.

Given this mutability of definitions and criteria of judgment in Max's world, it should not be surprising to find that "inappropriate" discourses need to be redeployed to supply interpretive hints for critics attempting to follow some of the ramifications of the film's postmodernity. For example, take and mutate this quote from academic art history: Max could be said to inhabit a "world peopled with signs, figures and emblems, where all objects and beings (including rational beings) exchange attributes and properties in a perpetual semantic shift."[3] This description is actually from Germain Bazin's classic study of the European Baroque, but it does apply very neatly to *Beyond Thunderdome*. Think of the transmogrifications worked by Max in his adaptation of the common fly-swatter for the purposes of self-defense; or consider his manipulation of the whistle which was originally disguised as a boot-brace and which later affords him salvage in the Thunderdome. Think also of the various names applied to Max: by his own assignation he is "Nobody"; by Aunty Entity's he is "Raggedy Man"; according to the children he is "Captain Walker"; in the Thunderdome he is "The Man with No Name," as well as the "Romantic Hero" (called "bad, beautiful and crazy," in echo of Lady Caroline Lamb's characterization of Lord Byron as "mad, bad and dangerous to know").

What is most intriguing about Bazin's quotation concerning the exchange of attributes and properties is that originally (before the semantic shift that I am working here) the sentence referred to the "transcendental world" that is recurrently evoked in seventeenth-century European painting and architecture. How is it that there can seem to be some formal *and* thematic similarities between contemporary Australia and late-Renaissance Europe? How can one era speak *to* and *of* the other?

To justify highlighting Bazin's words here, I contend that the postmodern, or "high contemporary" mentality that seems to prevail in *Beyond Thunderdome* has been formulated by social conditions similar to those obtaining in the baroque era when the world began to mean too much, when "every object embodied a message."[4] To explain such a complex time in schematic terms, the baroque sensibility could be said to have arisen out of an epistemological adjustment necessitated by several sea changes such as Europe's encounter with the "New World," the development of industrial printing, the higher incidence of widespread travel by writers and artists, and the rise of an economically influential bourgeoisie at the same time as the great European dynasties of artistic patronage were still able to sponsor memorials to themselves. It doesn't stretch feasibility too far to propose parallels between the intellectual tumult of the present day and the epistemological volatility of the baroque era.

The baroque sensibility was produced by a breakdown in discriminative criteria, but it also *celebrated* such "lawlessness." Baroque art and architecture, sponsored in the main by the church or the aristocracy (each in contention with the other for preeminence in this time of change), operated on a corporate aesthetic, celebrating the notion of agglomeration and hyperbolic ambition. For all its lust for power, however, the baroque was also animated by an imaginative vigor. For all its "monstrosity," the baroque existed to valorize creativity.

It was a transcendental aesthetic. A baroque artifact was always intended to be much more than the sum of its parts. It was meant to lead the viewer elsewhere.

There are enough similarities between baroque economics and aesthetics, on the one hand, and Kennedy-Miller's mode of production, on the other, to warrant pursuing the comparison. *Beyond Thunderdome* is one of the most expensive films ever produced in Australia, and the extravagance of its production values is so obvious that the prodigal expenditure of resources becomes a primary theme of the text, simply by virtue of how the film looks and sounds. The huge ensemble of actors, the far-flung locations, the array of machinery and massive sets, and the technically intricate camera movements that thread through the film were all possible only because Kennedy-Miller were in a sufficiently secure investment position to spend virtually whatever they needed to capture the required form. And this was a form signifying imperial ambition and creative exuberance, a form concerned with nation-building and the reassemblage of a culture undergoing fundamental adjustments. It is a baroque kind of form—an exuberant style entirely apposite to the themes of the film. The mood of celebration and humor that saturates *Beyond Thunderdome* from the first hurrah of the opening credits is a product of the filmmakers' delight in the sensuality, the plastic "fecundity," of cinema as a creative material. It is a mood, also, which testifies to a somewhat heartening faith in the possibilities of social reorganization in Australia. And if myths exist in order to convince us of contentions that cannot always be rationally supported, then *Beyond Thunderdome* must be a utopian myth of the cinema and of Australia.

Before becoming more specific, I will outline in abstract terms the baroque qualities that seem to operate in *Beyond*

Thunderdome. It is generally agreed that one of the defining qualities of the baroque is its compositional emphasis on exultation, release, or open-endedness. Germain Bazin attempts to translate this *élan* by detailing the configurations in Tintoretto's *Presentation of the Virgin in the Temple:*

> Tintoretto's composition [. . .] is dynamic. Space does not unfold in breadth but in depth; the surface is crossed by a violent spiral movement; its vector, so to speak, is the gesture of the woman in the foreground. [The woman points up a stairway to a vivid sky while encouraging a girl to take her first steps of ascension.] The action begins in front of the picture plane and continues behind it. The forms, indissolubly linked in an organic unity, are animated by a levitational force.[5]

It is a style in which "everything is designed to astonish,"[6] and regardless of whether the artist's imperative is anarchistic or utopian (in the case of Kennedy-Miller it is plainly more of the latter), one can hardly disagree with Judith Hook's contention that "baroque art [realizes] a freer sense of form," and that it is "often spiral in its movemeent, suggesting that the work of art will only be completed beyond its formal limits."[7]

It is not simply glib to draw attention to the word "beyond" when we bring these baroque notions to the third Mad Max film. Apart from the narrative, which drifts open-ended and saga-like through the trilogy, and through representational space, as the trilogy follows the fortunes of the "man who wandered out into the wasteland,"[8] *Beyond Thunderdome* is threaded together by the formal trope of the ascendant spiral. In the majority of shots in *Mad Max 1*, the camera is noticeably earthbound or downcast as it guns along in a storyline that has almost nothing to do with levity or transcendence. By way of contrast in *Beyond Thunderdome*, once the banshee swoop of Jedediah's flying machine has established the locale as the legendary desert, the film is buttressed predominantly with up-lifting crane shots. The ascendant camera-curve over the gates of Bartertown is the first of a series. From that moment on, the pattern of movement upward and beyond is established emphatically. Describing arcs all the way, the camera is impelled to Aunty's aerie where it swirls around Max and Aunty as they hedge and parry in a subliminal dance of courtship. Then, min-utes later the camera descends with Aunty into the Thun-derdome to record the gestural performance of the Ringmas-ter. Everything in his demeanor is expressive of movement upward and outward. As he twists, scans, and projects to wel-come the audience above him, he virtually announces the film's "vector" in preface to the gyrating, projectile movements of Max and Blaster in their deadly tryst.

The most eloquent of the film's baroque motifs occurs when Max's future must be decided by the spinning wheel of fortune. Even before it starts rotating, this symbol is pushed through several semantic shifts. When the radiant game-show hostess gestures the viewer into the theatre of fate, the wheel refers to an original context involving television programs from a previous culture. But the symbol twists almost immediately, with the realization that the TV game-shows took the wheel motif from a tradition of metaphysical iconography that spirals back through centuries. So, when Max chances his arm at the wheel, the formal logic established by the first twenty minutes of the film demands that the camera will pull up and away from the whirling ring that is to fling the hero into yet another state of becoming, *beyond* a stable personal order.

Most importantly, the film's "transcendental style" is not reserved solely for the Bartertown interlude. The "yondering" motifs pervade the entire narrative. Later, for example, among the children at The Crack in the Earth, most of the talk, and many of the crucial actions (including when Max throws Captain Walker's cap to the winds), are inspired by forces of levitation and flight. This spiritual vagrancy is embodied most emphatically in the plane that forms the sacred site of the children's folk religion. At almost every turn, the film aspires to take off.

Of course, with any move beyond a status quo, a new beginning is signalled. This is to say that the baroque configurations, the plastic exuberance, and the stylistic effervescence of *Beyond Thunderdome* are right and convincing for the telling of a new myth of origin.

With each fresh beginning an adaptation has to occur, or else nothing new has actually started. In new times there are new contexts, and all available signs must be freshly assayed. With each beginning, a novel story (which is not necessarily to say an *original* story) must be arranged from the knowledge, grammar and motifs at hand. The stories are required. They explain the state of things, past, present, and future.

"Open your book at page one," says the children's record. It keeps talking, and very soon it asks, "Where are you going?" Inevitably, the reply declaims, "I am going home." The record from the past keeps resonating with clues about how we might interpret Max's story. These notions of destiny and domesticity are crucial to the saga as it has been developed in its third installment.

So, the record asks, "Where are you going?" and the answer casts our minds back to earlier in the story, at the Crack in the Earth, when the children entreated Max, "We're ready, Captain Walker; take us home." But the message Max has brought them, the message he has carried since the trauma at the end of *Mad Max 1*, is that now, after all that has happened, you cannot go home again. You cannot rebuild without adapting old patterns. You must work with what is available, which includes the past. But you cannot *live* in the past. (In this respect, characterizations of Max as a modern Ulysses break down—Max has no Ithaca to lure him on and back.)

In the post-apocalyptic Australia that is conjured in *Beyond Thunderdome*, even historically validated notions of Australianness are no longer exclusively relevant. Although the film abounds with nationally specific icons, idioms, and leitmotifs, there are also a welter of *trans*national elements available as raw material for the reconstruction. On the occasion of a new beginning, nothing can be counted foreign or ill-fitted to the environment if it happens to be there, existing or surviving. Hence the presence of so much that would once have been counted "alien": the monkey; the camels; Max himself dressed in Bedouin garb; the Mel Gibson star-persona with his well-publicized Irish-American-Australian sense of patriality; Tina Turner in all her black Americanness and with all her legends of past survivals and rejuvenations; the exotic name of Savannah accorded to the girl who will tell the stories that will define the future. It is significant also that Savannah's second name is Nix, an austral-English word to put one in mind of starting from scratch. All these characters and characteristics need not be uniformly admired, but they can be counted foreign only if you still believe in the definitions and judgments that prevailed before The Change—if you still believe you can go home again, if you still believe in an English Australia. Indeed, this question of how to incorporate "foreignness" is fundamental to any redefinition of Australian culture in the last years of the twentieth century. And that, after all, is one of the things that *Beyond Thunderdome* is most emphatically about.

The roads that rifled through *Mad Max 1* do not exist in the third film. There are only trails blazed at the moment of wandering. Admittedly, there is also the railroad track, a relic of an old order. But, as the denouement emphasizes, the train leads nowhere hopeful beyond Bartertown. (I am presuming that it is agreed that the film clearly presents Bartertown as the wrong new start. As Max tells the children, the two places to avoid are the "the nothing" tracts of the desert, where humanity is of no value, and Bartertown, where humanity is no more valuable than a million other commodities.) The direction taken, therefore, must be informed by novelty and adaptation. In short, outmoded myths must be bastardized or left behind.

The Mad Max films have been so influential in Australian cultural history because they have set out to adapt one of the most enduring local myths: that of the transcendent failure. Even until the 1970s, the legends of Sturt, Eyre, Leichhardt (and Voss, their fictional apotheosis), Burke and Wills, Pharlap, Les Darcy, and the ANZACs were still required by white Australia. For just under two hundred years, as the environment (and in the case of the ANZACs, the world) continued to rebuff the "advances" of Anglo-Australian civilization even as the culture persisted in its conquistadorial attitudes, myths were needed to rationalize, or to "naturalize," the continuous stalemate. For veracity's sake the myth had to be cognizant of the failures of the culture of dominion. But, for esteem's sake, some kind of glory had to be "explained into" the futility. As long as the conquistadorial attitude was not renounced, the unrequited outcome of the project had to be regarded as romantically uplifting. When a quester pursues a myth as far as it can be taken, and he still receives no reward, then the failure itself must be mythologized, naturalized, and rendered ennobling and emotionally sustaining.

Since the 1980s, however, the imperatives behind this grand tradition seem to have altered. Success has become a popular theme—in beer commercials, corporate-raiding adventures, and highly selective celebrations of sporting triumphs. The battler has been superseded by a far sleeker, better groomed, and motivationally primed individual. Even Kennedy-Miller, after *The Dismissal, Vietnam* and *Bodyline* had sought to develop a critical understanding of disillusionment and humility, have more recently concentrated on stories valorizing achievement—most melodramatically in *Dirtwater Dynasty* and *Bangkok Hilton*, but also very pragmatically in the success story of *The Clean Machine* which climaxes with *achievement* in the same narrative terrain where Robert Caswell's *Scales of Justice* opted for melancholia five years earlier.

So, the grand tradition of the heroic failure is on the wane. And it is tempting to assert that the Mad Max trilogy could well have been one of the principal factors in The Change. Certainly one can interpret *Mad Max 1* as a spectacular valediction to 1970s Australia: Max begins his saga relaxed in casual domesticity, in a beach house adorned with raw pine, batik, and hippy-bourgeois bric-a-brac, but his "lifestyle" is terminally seared by a "devolving" world that he cannot opt out of. More specifically, given that the Mad Max films deal explicitly in the symbology of Australian landscape, one can argue that the trilogy analyzes the myths of failure by dramatizing white society's traditional conflicts with the land.

The trilogy can be read, then, as a chronicle of the collective loss of faith in the drive to conquer the environment. Max can be seen to be a once orthodox, law-abiding suburbanite who is now on a journey of education. He is a likable yob who has had change thrust upon him, and he is now learning to live again by adapting his vision and his aspirations. Granted, *Beyond Thunderdome* concludes with Max still a failure (in the tradition of Leichhardt et al.) insofar as he still cannot return from his self-transcendent wanderings with any palpable prize, grace, or answers. He is still defining himself through negation: finally, yet again, he abjures society's pleasures along with its responsibilities. In these respects, Kennedy-Miller are still riding with the narrative energies contained in the waning myths. But more significantly, Max has survived; he has succeeded in *living*, rather than in *escaping*, Voss-like, into apotheosis. Max is learning and adapting. He is moving beyond the strictures of his heritage.

The trauma that blighted Max's life at the end of the first installment has forced him to move. When we first catch sight of him in *The Road Warrior*, he has already undergone change—he has given up trying to police the land, trying to coerce it to his law. Nor does he ever hanker again to return to his old role—in *Beyond Thunderdome* it is the burghers of Bartertown, not Max, who repeatedly invoke The Law. Having abandoned his adversarial attitude to the environment—having left the road—Max has begun to trace the contours of the continent, reading it a little more cannily, moving according to its dictates, and growing from it. Once The Change has occurred, he even encounters the odd renegade who is operating similarly. In *The Road Warrior*, for example, Bruce Spence's character wins Max's grudging respect by erupting in a geyser of red earth to get the jump on him. The successful characters are now the ones who are incorporated in the environment.

Max's adaptation continues in the third film, as evidenced in his desert clothing, his ingeniously customized camel train, and his now unquestionable status as an expert in the ways of the land. He is becoming one kind of native. Moreover, as a happy complication, he is also beginning to need society again, and he has started to ask about strategies for the future. "What's the plan?" he says to the convict after they have fled Bartertown. "Plan?" replies the convict, much to Max's droll chagrin. "There aint no plan!" Even more rehabilitative in its implications, Max glimpses, and *wants*, the chance to build a new community with the children from The Crack in the Earth.

But most pointedly, Max has not yet earned or learned happiness and security in Changed Australia. He's still out there in the wasteland. Indeed, as the bandage on his leg indicates, he is still carrying the immobilizing wound that he received when his world was defiled at the end of the first film. He has not yet recovered from the trauma. There remains an arid, fearful kind of celibacy afflicting the hero. In the second film, Papagallo's tribe attempt to persuade Max to come with them to "Paradise," where there'll be "nothing to do but bree-e-e-d": he declines the invitation, with a hint of embarrassment and an almost hermetic taciturnity. In the third film, the faintest of sparks glint between Max and Aunty, particularly when the romantic saxophone refrain which Jess had played in *Mad Max 1* heralds their first meeting in the aerie. But ultimately it comes to nothing more than a husky *double entendre* from her and a faintly bemused glance from him.

Even so, the affection and the humorous cooperation that he achieves with the children indicate that he might almost be ready to override his affliction and move on to subjective success rather than take solace in a tradition of transcendent failure. In the prologue to *Mad Max 2* the audience is told that Max had wandered out into the wasteland and that "it was here, in this blighted place, that he learned to live again." *Beyond Thunderdome* maintains this theme of reanimation, highlighting Max's vital ability to keep moving. The logical project for *Mad Max 4,* should it ever eventuate, would be to show Max learning to *love* again. There are myths aplenty to commandeer for that theme, but the difficulty would be to maintain the sense of chill that creeps into the epilogue of the third film when the breath of mawkishness bubbling through the children's return home is bated by the deathly quiet images of Sydney rotting after the nuclear winter.

This prompts another question which ought to prompt another essay: given the cataclysm that Max has lived through, could it ever be plausible, or even ethical, to portray him as happy?

9

Remembering Art

There is a school of thought (and I'm enrolled in it) maintaining that a critic is not primarily concerned with providing answers. Rather, the critic's job is to ask the most useful questions. If there is still some pertinence in I.A. Richards's celebrated quip that "a book is a machine to think with," then a critic might be the mechanic of such mental engineering. Moreover, this is not necessarily a completely cerebral process: the critic should be the first person to acknowledge that one can think, learn, and know *emotionally* without necessarily abandoning the intellectual's role. Nor am I discussing a specialized occupation here, for just as everybody is a thinker, so *all* readers have the right to regard themselves as critics.

And in the particular milieu of the visual arts, all *viewers* ought to be critics. (It's not a long way from here to the next connection, which proposes that all viewers are readers, but this is another set of questions.)

When confronted with so much of contemporary culture that is patently concerned with "quotation," "appropriation," "image-scavenging," "cultural rag-picking," "sign retrieval," and so on, most critics have tended to ask two questions: Is there anything original to be praised here? and What does it all mean? Useful enough questions. The one about originality is at the top of the agenda these days, with copyright so obviously untenable in philosophical as well as legal terms. The consumer-led support of larcenous aesthetics in local independent film and video, and in the international hip-hop (a subset of rap music) and house music industries over the last five years indicates that copyright (and its attendant belief in the pristine artistic imagination) is now popularly acknowledged to be anachronistic.

However, there is at least one other intriguing query to be raised about much of the "reprocessing" that is occurring in contemporary Western culture. Rather than Who owns it? or What does it mean? one could ask *How* does it mean? How is it that this "uneven," "multi-layered," "cross-cultural," or "intertextual" work appeals to its viewer? If you respond to a piece by Peter Tyndall or Juan Davila, for example, *how* has that response come about?

This is a useful question precisely because it sets you thinking in several directions. And any single line of inquiry is inevitably not conclusive or exhaustive. (Such infinitude of argument is not a problem once it is acknowledged. The acknowledgment simply prompts further enquiry.) So when I trace just one line of thought now, it's nothing like the last word. It's hardly even an introduction to the kinds of thinking that works such as Davila's should be setting in play.

For the brief duration of this chapter, I'd like to concentrate on one train of thought. I want to examine the traditional discipline of mnemonics, or artificial memory-systems, in order to suggest that much contemporary art is engaged in a program to preserve, activate, and refine an inherently unstable social construct that we can call "popular memory."

Systematic mnemonics date back at least 2,050 years to an anonymous Latin text called *Ad Herennium* which sets out the techniques by which dense and complex patterns of knowledge could be memorized and thus kept current in the minds of practitioners of the art of memory. Of course, in an oral-based culture such as ancient Rome, it was imperative that a significant number of citizens were able to memorize all manner of information so that the corpus of knowledge activating that society was not in danger of debilitation. Outside the tiny elite of citizens who could write and read in such a society, memory was the "place" where popular knowledge lived or died.

In the classic *ars memoria* described in *Ad Herennium*, the custodians of knowledge are advised to "locate" their ideas in a spatial pattern within their own minds. Notions are to be arranged according to the structural logic of the pattern visualized. For example, if the custodian chooses to "lay out" the elements of a treatise according to the shape of a well-known building, such as the city's temple, then the "introductory" concept is mentally coded as an image and then placed on the steps to the building. The first major development of argument is visualized and placed at the entrance portal; tangential discourses are found to the left and right, in particular shrines and alcoves beside the main aisle. As the argument advances, the structure of the discourse thus takes on a "solid," unforgettable shape. As Frances Yates explains in her definitive text on the topic: "We have to think of the ancient orator as moving in imagination through his memory building *whilst* he is making his speech, drawing from the memorised places the images he has placed on them. The method ensures that the points are remembered in the right order."[1]

Most significantly, architecture was never construed as the only effective "mold" for the information. Throughout the fifteenth and sixteenth centuries, for example, practitioners of the *ars memoria* commonly utilized the zodiac as the structuring pattern. Moreover, an aesthetic tradition dating back to Aristotle indicated that paintings, drawings, or sculptures also could logically be employed as prompts for mental information. In *De Anima* Aristotle maintained that "it is impossible even to think without a mental picture." And memory, he continued, "is a collection of mental pictures from sense impressions, but with a time element added."[2]

The seeds of Aristotelian speculation on memory flourished in Europe during the sixteenth and seventeenth centuries (culminating in the extreme visualist bias of eighteenth-century science and philosophy[3]). A profusion of Renaissance memory treatises advised readers either to set their notions onto a well-beloved preexistent image or to draw an original picture shaped to the special pattern of their information. As an example of the first option, in 1562 Ludovico Dolce suggested that all students of classical mythology would do well to memorize their primary texts by referring to the paintings of Titian.[4] Or, to exemplify the second variant in a way Frances Yates has suggested, there may be a plausible mnemonic explanation for the intricate grotesque figures that illuminate so many medieval and Renaissance manuscripts: the images may be densely coded visual summaries of the arguments presented in the contiguous texts. The elements of the discourse are broken down into the several related components of the drawing and then remembered during the process of recalling the body of knowledge to one's mind.

Similarly, as Jacky Redgate's photographic series "From the Book of Painting" has indicated, visual works such as the paintings of Pieter Breughel can be interpreted as catalysts for remembering a complex unwritten culture, the system in Breughel's case being Flemish folktales and proverbs. In a community not equipped with the "storage" capacity of a widespread written culture, the details of an oral canon must be insured against disappearance: the Flemish folk paintings had such a preservative function. Or to cite an example from closer to home, it is plausible to understand some of the functions of traditional Aboriginal painting as mnemonic insofar as the works are visual codifications of crucial elements of the dreaming (a system of stories crammed with spiritual information that is also meteorological, geographical, dietary, and so on) pertaining to the region that the paintings depict and embellish.

The "problem" paintings of Tim Johnson refer to this question of *how* a work of art is used. Some of Johnson's images take on the appearance of the works of Aboriginal painters from the Papunya Tula, others bear resemblance to Tibetan landscapes, while some meld the two aesthetics. By featuring these speciously "exotic" styles, the painter nudges the interpretation of the imagery in a particular direction, toward issues vital to colonized societies in many regions of the globe, issues of communal memory and traditional lore and how to hold on to them while a consuming culture encroaches.

Of course the paintings are also tangled in the vexed question about which side of the hegemony a white painter using Aboriginal forms is liable to be on. The answer is not likely to be simple, but Johnson opts to work in an inevitably controversial area: plenty of mud will be slung, and fair dollops of it will stick. It's not a "clean" area of cultural history that he's operating in. Indeed, this suggests another theme of the paintings: how can one begin to negotiate an equitable cultural liaison between white and black societies. Given that Johnson's work can evoke bitter condemnation as well as enthusiasm, the works can be made useful if they are treated as testaments to the debts to be paid in the trade between an imperious culture and an Aboriginal society that is staunchly resistant, but also culturally generous—after all Johnson's dot-style paintings exist only because of tutelage received at the Papunya Tula.

But to return to the first-mentioned aspects of Johnson's paintings, they signal that they are concerned with the processes by which systems of lore and information are maintained. They designate memory as a major theme. The memory of *what*, precisely, is not explicitly designated (as in Redgate's photographs also). But specific as this question is, it is subsidiary to the principal concern or "problem" of how to formulate and sustain a coherent body of science, intuition, history, ethics, or wisdom perhaps, in a society whose values and limits have become inevitably fluid. The paintings are concerned more with evoking a sensation akin to *deja vu* as the viewer responds to the aesthetic "rightness" of the composition that unifies pictorial elements which, separately presented, may seem totally unrelated. The paintings are thus concerned with activating a desire to remember. They are not recording the substantive details of any particular memory. Inappropriate as it might seem at first, Johnson's work could take as its epigraph the same maxim that E. M. Forster used in *Howard's End:* "Only connect!"

Given that Australia is a nation constituted out of a myriad cultures and epistemologies which, viewed outside a humanist set of presumptions about "the family of man," could feasibly be counted incommensurable, it is not surprising that much artwork produced in this country is explicitly concerned with the problem of hybridizing an aesthetic out of sundry available traditions. Nor is it surprising that a society comprised of so many constituents with family memories of exile and displacement should give rise to so many artists concerned with the workings of memory.

On the understanding that two of the definitive concerns of postmodernism are now recognized to be a preoccupation with historiographical problems and a fascination with creole cultures, it is logical that several younger local artists could be promoted on the art market as exemplary postmodernists. And, of course, the theme of memory—particularly popular memory—is integral to the historiographical concerns of international postmodernism. Which brings this essay back to its analysis of mnemonics as they are evinced in contemporary Australian art.

Curiously enough, postmodernism's preoccupation with questions of memory has not been discussed very often in terms of mnemonics. The keyword has tended to be "allegory:" postmodernism is often described as "an allegorical practice." Now, if we were to think of, say, Dante's *Divine Comedy* as a treatise laid out like a memory-prompt about the ethical and metaphysical universe of early-Renaissance Europe, we could see how the allegory is a literary form adaptable to the purposes of the memory-system. Then, insofar as *visual* mnemonics can be construed as the pictorial analogue of a literary allegory such as *The Divine Comedy*, the critical interest in postmodernism as an allegorical practice begins to make sense. The term "allegory" has drifted over from its primarily literary niche to find a privileged place in the glossary of contemporary art criticism. The kink in the word's lineage can distract us from the likelihood that in the context of the visual arts, "mnemonic" might be a more informative word to apply to much contemporary "appropriative" work.

But still there is the question, *how* might these pictures be functioning mnemonically? My contention is that, nowadays, in a Western culture in which the nonwritten discourses of television, video, radio, and cinema are so pervasive, information is not containable in any single space or system. For at least three centuries after the development of industrial printing, oral culture and its "unstable" corpus of knowledge were perceived to be moribund and of diminishing importance in comparison to the confident, progressive coherence of a scientific worldview served by empirical methods of recording. However, now, with the proliferation of the electronic media and with increasing philosophical interrogation of the notion of objective truth, a new oral culture obtains. It is a culture bloated with information, more information than can be contained in one recording system or in one mind. It is a culture which must select its preferred truths from all the stories and worldviews available.

Let me exemplify the change, quickly: at the time of the Enlightenment, when printing presses were proliferating all over Europe, the setting down of *all* the world's secular knowledge seemed both a rational and a feasible project; yet, nowadays, the idea of a comprehensive encyclopedia seems chimerical, if not laughable. Once, the world contained all the knowledge that could possibly exist; nowadays, innumerable possible worlds contend for existence within the unstable, expansive universe of information. (It should be emphasized that the power-laden world of written culture has not been supplanted or subverted. But potent, concomitant worlds now operate alongside and in interaction with the "clerical" system of knowledge.)

A participant in today's massmedia culture can hope to become competent, but never consummate, in the evaluation, interpretation, and transmission of the available data. As a corollary to this overabundance, a style of art has become widespread. It has developed simply because it is needed. It consists of conglomerate images devised to some extent as memory-prompts. (Indeed, a day in the company of a radio in any Western metropolis indicates that conglomerate *sounds* are also being deployed mnemonically, particularly in the cut-up, sampling, and dub of the many subgenres of contemporary dance music.)

It is an art-style with functional similarities to the industrial film still. Movie producers initially commission still photographs for the purposes of first-release sales promotion of their product. However, once the business of promotion is complete, the stills fulfill their other function: they become catalysts to our recalling the complexities of the film when we are attempting to think our way through the "big movie" of a mass-mediated life.

A good deal of contemporary visual art is engaged in a similar project. Such images cannot be construed as containers of information. Rather, they are suggestive distillations of "highly charged" portions of massmedia experience *combined with* the equally rich and complex legacy of printed stories, philosophy, and history bequeathed to contemporary professional artists during their educational "apprenticeships" in academies all over the world. Moreover, a participant in the oversupplied capitalist culture can be assured that if there are still realms of shared experience in the pluralist West, then one of the arenas of this commonality is likely to be the mass media.

But there is no way to certify which *particular* aspects of media experience are the common moments shared by a significant majority of people participating in the culture. The images therefore are not to be construed as simple metaphors as if they were practical resumés of more complex, but comprehensibly regulated, bodies of knowledge. Rather, they are anaphors, tropes that do nothing more than point toward the volume of information from which they are derived and to which they refer, tropes whose meanings are not tied down securely but take their tenor from the contexts in which they are being deployed. If the images are distillations, they are by definition inadequate or partial distillations. They are there to jog one's memories of the world of meaning that has passed by daily in the environment of mediated information and entertainment. If the larger system of experience means nothing to the viewer, then there is nothing for the viewer to remember when standing in front of the picture, and, therefore, there is probably little "value" to be discerned in the picture itself. (It is apposite to recall here that the aphorism appended to Jacky Redgate's *A Portrait Chronicle of Photographs, England* was a quotation attributed to Walter Benjamin: "Every image from the past that is not recognised by the present as one of its own concerns, threatens to disappear irretrievably.")

When standing in front of a picture by, say, Maria Kosic, you can't expect to *transcend* your mundane world. On the contrary, you *recollect* the environment of ideas, beliefs, and preconceptions that you inhabit in a society washed by information that cannot be efficiently contained. This emphasis on recollection rather than transcendence is one way in which much contemporary visual art has abjured the modernism proselytized by the school of Clement Greenberg.

Of course, it is not just *any* image that can function effectively as anaphor. The "commemorative" artist must choose and combine and represent images in such a way that they "over-signify." That is to say the images must not yield up their meanings immediately and simply. Admittedly this may sound like a standard definition of the aesthetic dimension celebrated by proponents of a "transcendent" modernist art, but the crucial difference in the case of a mnemonic practice is that the "excess" of signification directs the viewer not into a rarified realm beyond meaning, but out to *more* meaning elsewhere, in other related media and discourses that also give rise to meanings.

The anaphors selected and reworked by the mnemonic artist must be intensely meaningful. Taken separately, each element may be banal or thrilling, or both. The artist and the viewer work with their "flashes" of memory to reconstitute them into a combination which *means*, which *makes sense*. Accordingly, even the banal or the disquieting or the distasteful anaphor can be a component in a thrilling work of art if the combination of the constituent parts is such that unexpected insights, surprising thoughts, emotions, or even opinions temporarily forgotten, arise as a result of the viewing.

So, it is inaccurate to describe mnemonic art as merely critical, deconstructive, or spiritless (to choose just three options from the glossary of pejorative terminology). In well formulated mnemonic work there is an undeniable element of vitality and celebration for those viewers with the memory to use it.

Memorial art can also be described as "melodramatic," an adjective which many people might find pejorative, but which refers to a mode that is critically neglected despite its prevalence in so many facets of contemporary culture. As Peter Brooks notes in his authoritative book on the subject, the crucial aspect of melodrama occurs in the moment of "mute gesture" or "inarticulate cry" when the text changes register either in an instant of overstated, "extreme" expression, or in a declension to bathos or banality which takes on meaning by virtue of its being contextualized as "art." Rather than spotlighting some perceived inadequacy of language (or of "art"), melodrama in this moment summons the potentialities of communication; it seeks to encompass the complexity of its topic by pointing across media, genres, and language-systems to a continuing transtextual search for significance. Accordingly, Brooks says, melodramatic art does not emphasize any poverty of language. Rather it partakes of an "expressive ambition" characteristic of the early Romantics—most notably Rousseau and Sade—who were obsessed by the idea that they must say all: that nothing of the possible human response must be left unexpressed, that writing must be a continual overstatement.[5]

There is a way of interpreting the melodramatic project, therefore, as an attempt to deal with a breadth of knowledge and a system of information which have become uncontainable. So, to relate this theory to the art of making sense of contemporary experience, I suggest that an effective postmodern image is one that evokes more memories than it actually contains; it is an image that prompts the retrieval of information from a much larger field of knowledge at the same time as it works to present itself as a concentrated miniature archive of contemporary information. The postmodernism worth our interest promotes the process of historical research and analysis at the same time as it makes of itself a project that documents the contemporary. Each useful postmodern image is a memory-system to be used to make sense of the present so as to guarantee coherence for the future. Only in this temporal ubiquity can a postmodern image be usefully deemed transcendent.

10

Elsewhere, Today. 2 False Starts about 4 Australian Artists

Writing around the Work of Jacky Redgate,

Robyn Stacey, Jeff Gibson, and

Anne Zahalka

I. Elsewhere

During these years he met his seminars,
went & lectured & read, talked with human beings,
paid insurance & taxes:
but his mind was not on it. His mind was elsewheres
in an area where the soul not talks but sings
& where foes are attacked with axes.

This is an excerpt from No. 352 of John Berryman's *The Dream Songs*, a gigantic verse sequence in which the American poet reveals the history, memories, fears, and fantasies of Henry, a complex semiautobiographical persona dedicated to the ideal of living poetically throughout his unstable twentieth-century life. Henry is a hero both tragic and comic, deliberately pursuing a life of rebuttal and frustration while confidently accruing moments of intense joy and insight in his middle-American milieu of Minnesota. He scrutinizes his mundane habitat, and he often finds himself celebrating the ordinary in extraordinary epiphanies of percipience or willful self-delusion. But even so, he aches all the time to transcend the inanities and cruelties of his domestic banality. More often than not, his mind is elsewhere.

By his own admission, Henry is a fool, an equation that cannot be balanced. He knows about insurance and taxes, he divines incongruities in his aspirations and personal capabilities, he details the incapacities of his self and his society, but he steadfastly plots his course toward a land of musing, where the soul not talks but sings.

Henry has knowledge enough of himself and his times to admit that such romanticism is probably untenable nowadays. He knows that within his fantasyland, axes are flailing to good and bad effect, always threatening to sever the ties of acceptance and understanding between himself and his neighbors. But despite his facility for worldliness, he believes in the process—the means, if not necessarily the ends—of dreaming. He finds an occupation—not just a distraction—in following the startling jumps of association, remembrance, and intention yielded by a mind consciously directed to muse. Berryman makes of the reverie a life for himself. One of his own choosing: Henry's life.

As many of the dream songs emphasize, Henry yearns to feel at home. (Once or twice he accords himself a family name: Henry House.) But it's a mobile home that he needs. Henry repeatedly draws attention to his national heritage, but he does so not to fix his identity immutably in one place and one history. He is not *incumbent* as an American artist. Rather, he is colonial, still a tenant, not a native in the place where he lives. His hereditary tree might reach down through American generations, but sooner or later it finds root elsewhere—in Europe. And if he is to occupy himself as an artist, his work must seek some of its definition in traditions from "foreign" realms, regardless of whether he casts himself as an ally or an adversary (or perhaps an orphan) of the parental culture of Europe.

If ever you wanted to understand the tides on any particular shoreline, you would need to know the contours of the beach and its sandbanks, but you would also need to look to the moon. It is a similar process of orientation, a kind of cultural trigonometry, that Henry practices. He can hope to know where he is only by referring to where he is not. He is habitually analyzing himself even as he is dreaming. By directing his muse elsewhere—to the places of his beginnings as well as to the fields of future possibilities—he is simultaneously dismantling and creating his identity in his daily work.

Surprisingly enough, Henry's American divinations point to some of the preconditions—geographical, historical, psychic, and aesthetic—of an Australian spiritual vagrancy. In any "new world," an immigrant may want to feel at home, but from so many points of view one can attain such grace only by looking away from the base that one craves.

In this respect, Henry and the vagabond concerns of *The Dream Songs* can help us get our bearings when we try to apprehend some of the preoccupations in the photographs before us here. As we approach this variegated assemblage of works by Australian artists who are pondering particular notions of displacement, discontinuity, and realignment in so many realms (geographical, national, psychic, and aesthetic)

Henry might seem a fellow traveler. His errant musings on his private identity and his national allegiance emphasize the vital question subtending this Australian work: how can one begin to feel composed and at home?

A great deal of Australian art and historiography has been devoted to the definition of innate qualities of life in this country. It is a process of finding or fabricating a sense of place for a non-Aboriginal society. It is part of a process of nation building. Certainly, the nationalist contention that a region and a nation are destined for one another is strategically useful at several stages in the maturation of a colonial society. The belief that the spirit of a place will rise up to define and direct a society can be effective voodoo to a waning administrative power struggling to keep the hearts and minds of the dominion in thrall. Indeed, nationalist incantations have often galvanized anti-British forces in Australia throughout the past two centuries. But just as surely, nationalism is currently being deployed in Australia, in these times of Bicentennial "celebrations" and economic rationalizations, as a clampdown on the myriad unorthodox factions and fictions that proliferate here.

Nationalism at present is the cultural strategy which most effectively disenfranchises the indecorous and dissatisfied communities inhabiting the island. In the context of "celebrations" such as the Bicentenary or the sundry sporting ceremonies that roll around annually, factional agitation and criticism are deemed meanminded and self-pitying. There is something especially invidious about this cajoling, condescending method of authorizing middle-Australia as natural, fun-loving, confident, . . . and *unified*.

In TV advertisements (conjuring and targeting a manageable *national* market), in newspaper interviews and features,

Royal Visits, and public festivals, and in monumental architec-
tural commissions and multimedia "historical entertainments,"
the governmental culture in Australia is currently attempting
to authorize the nation as an *achieved fact*, as a society stabilized
under the rule of compliant self-definition. The jingoism is
so pervasive, so environmental, at present, that it is difficult
to attain a critical distance on it all. The rhetoric required to
debunk the chauvinism behind the celebrations is more duplicitous than the straightforward empiricism that one can
marshal to expose the more archaic and brutal methods of social control (both explicit and implicit) that are also still being
enacted on outsider castes such as the Aboriginal population.
(This is not to say that the discriminative violence against
blacks is now being curtailed, or that exposure of the oppression is now any less imperative: on a pro rata basis, for example, the deaths of Aborigines in police custody are propor-
tionately higher than in South Africa.) With regard to the
"celebrations," the nationalist rationale attempts to preempt
any caviling voices by implying that it is churlish to complain
when the dinner table has been stacked and the guests are coming to the party to bear witness to the health of the nation.
But, vulgar as it is to say so, one cannot deny that the guest
list has been thoroughly vetted and that the Bicentennial nation is only one exclusive entity vying for the space and power
to live here.

The point to be made now is that if definitions of what
it means to work in and on Australian culture must be formulated (and definitions *are* useful, albeit definitively temporary,
in the process of finding one's bearings and assessing one's
standing), then a nationalist representation of the societies living here is currently highly dubious if one is allied to the unorthodox, the venturesome, and the different in Australia. If one

chooses to talk about the "Australian" qualities of a culture, the discussion needs to take account of the myriad "external" influences on life here, influences which are arbitrary, ideological, and political, and which have almost nothing to do with notions of eternal, essential, or natural Australian characteristics. Sooner rather than later, therefore, one is obliged to refute the organicist thesis of Australian historiography, which argues that the land will give rise to the nation.

Admittedly, the climate, the vegetation, the landscape—everything we designate "nature"—do give life a particular tone in any place. But the entity called "nature" is meaningful only in the context of the cultural patterns that are constantly being negotiated in a society. It is in terms of the nature of a society's understanding of itself that I would like to begin to ponder the images featured throughout this essay, for they call for redefinitions of the idea of Australia in relation to the notion of nature.

I will treat this idea more fully in the second half of the essay, but the point to be emphasized here is that if one expects the images to be *classically* Australian, they will refract the vision of their beholder. These works are concerned to "take on" the external forces that impinge on the configuration of Australian culture. Such forces are myriad, but for the moment we could focus our attention on three sets of concerns: (1) "Old World" preconceptions concerning "New Worlds"; (2) European aesthetic and ethical traditions; and (3) the photographic formats of international image-circulation and textual dissemination. Nowadays, these "un-Australian" preoccupations cannot be avoided when one begins to build artifacts in this country. The pictures in this chapter treat such external forces as inherent rather than alien to any culture produced here at the end of the twentieth century.

As long as Europeans have imagined a South Land, the outside influences on Australian society have been inherent to life here. In this sense, alien cultural factors must be counted definitively Australian. Hence it is that the artists in this essay focus much of their attention on the memorabilia, bric-a-brac, decorums, and poses that non-Aboriginal Australians have always imported into this country in an effort to make a home for themselves. This "stuff" is a collection of markers by which vagrants might get a sense of orientation, a sense at least of where they came from and of what they are at liberty to maintain and relinquish. And if this means that the possible definitions of nationality in Australia are as myriad as the cultures of the world, all the better in these times of the "celebration of the nation." If this means that "the nation" must be acknowledged to be an incommensurable diaspora, this should be perturbing only to an incumbent faction which would like to be regarded as *the* nation.

Here, then, is a collection of Australian images which question their constitution. The works might be deemed "Australian," but, in order to be so, they look away from their immediate locales in order to find their derivations and their destinations. If they have been constructed in a place called "Australia," the pictures indicate that in many respects and for several reasons, such a place must be regarded as "noplace."

And in the end, if one ponders these national images and one still needs to arrive at an idea of a singular Australia, one could ponder a quote from another Henry (Henry Miller) no less blessed or cursed than Berryman's: "Our destination is never a place but rather a new way of looking at things."

II. Today

> Today
> Oh! kangaroos, sequins, chocolate sodas!
> You really are beautiful! Pearls,
> harmonicas, jujubes, aspirins! all
> the stuff they've always talked about
> still makes a poem a surprise!
> These things are with us every day
> even on beacheads and biers. They
> do have meaning. They're strong as rocks.

Why is it that each time I try to make a start about Australian culture, I come up with a quote from a dead American poet?

Part of the answer must pertain to the conditions of cultural life in an import-society. (I trust it is not simply a reflex response to the kangaroos that Frank O'Hara uses here to spring his rhythm.) Part of the answer must lie in the way you get used to commandeering whatever drifts through your ambit when there is no singular, exclusive institution or epistemology ruling your musing.

Now that British Australia is becoming more of a memory than a regime and new administrative powers are contending for sovereignty, the classifications of culture ("high," "low," and "non-") that were in force during "the raj" have lost much of their clarity and cogency at the popular level. (Old Taste still hangs on in some Academies, Museums, and Newspapers, but patrician arguments for the leavening qualities of art are appearing increasingly anachronistic at a time when the most passionate, ingenious, and *persuasive* cultural work is coming out of radios, magazines, TV sets, film projectors, and small exhibition venues rather than institutional galleries.) Hence, while various newer factions contend for the citizens' hearts and minds, profane and profligate medleys of influences such as Merry Melodies cartoons, modernist American verse, photographic advertising tactics, the contradictory taxonomies of Linnaeus, Monboddo, and Darwin, the decor and personae of midday movies, the private histories of millions of migrant families, and "exotic" philosophies at odds with the traditions of British empiricism and commonsense, all such phenomena become available, *almost* divested of their previous connotations, *almost* "uncooked" as raw material for the contemporary artisan.

This is not to say that such material is presently unclassifiable or leeched of meaning. Rather, now that the socioeconomic dynamics of Australia are being refigured, intellectuals are obliged (or are at liberty) to select and combine the elements of their creativity according to aesthetics and scholarly traditions which would once have been considered unorthodox or impeachable within the art industry in Australia. Artists and intellectuals have begun to trade in the storehouses of the import-culture that has arisen as various regimes flow in to fill the vacuum left by the waning of British authority here after the Second World War.

Admittedly, this sounds like the rhetoric of institutional postmodernism as it operates in the international cultural market. And there is no denying the susceptibility of the idea of Australia to the discourses of "wildstyle" culture. But the point to be emphasized is that this susceptibility has arisen through the processes of more than two centuries of European-Australian history.

Many artists in Australia are now alloying innumerable traditions from the Old World, from Asia and the Pacific, as well as from "Newer Worlds" such as the syndicated newsagencies and the televisual universes. Indeed, so many Australian artists are adept at this "postmodernism" precisely because such "mongrel aesthetics" derive from the survival strategies developed in colonial dominions wherein all "matter" found at the site of exile must be *acculturated*, or rendered meaningful and useful. In this respect, white Australian culture has always been "wildstyle"; it exists because of its ability to redefine and work on whatever it finds to be nature. This is to say that postmodernism has a history (called "colonialism"), just as nations do.

Depending on how one classifies Australian nature, therefore, there are several political attitudes contending in the processes of acculturation. In the more orthodox accounts of landscape culture in Australian historiography, for example, the assumption that the land equals nature which equals, in turn, raw material, masks the irrefutable fact that the continent was an intricate artifact, culturally adorned and maintained by Aborigines, long before the incursion of Europe. By extension, any determination to regard the continent itself as the soil out of which the nation will grow, legitimizes a "horticultural" model of national culture, in which healthy, fully formed seedlings from elsewhere are thought to be transplanted into the new environment to develop into local varieties of approved culture. Implicit to this attitude is the idea that certain strains of culture (for example, the "proven" European ones that espouse heroic confrontation with the savage and the pristine) are essential to responsible artistic husbandry. Hence we inherit the idea that critics and artists alike must be ever vigilant to weed out corrupt and mutant strains which might reduce national culture to some global lowest common denominator. This is the rhetoric favored by people who would still find it useful to assert the differences between "High Art" and "low culture." Depending on what gets defined as legitimate raw material for creativity, therefore, culture can be certified either as "high," "true", and "sacred," or as "corrupt," "profane," and "low." By implication, true art is brave, pioneering, and energetic, while low art is lazy and craven in its "contentment" to deal with prefabricated signs and materials.

However, the distinction between nature art and low art can be shown to be specious, based as it is on the fallacy that nature and the imagination can be understood as if they were pristine or uncompromised by the values inherent to the culture of the beholder. Because we can perceive and understand it, nature is already culture. Or, equally applicable: all existing culture is, effectively, nature. Show me a piece of nature that is not already a sign! Show me a sign that doesn't deserve to be ploughed back into the fields of culture!

I make this challenge because I know I can't lose, and I'm serving my own vested interests. I want to resist the class which would maintain that fidelity to an English heritage is still the paramount virtue of "true" culture in Australia. I want to assert that the idea of "nature" is traditionally employed in Australia to laud the achievements of an established anglophone class which pioneered the re-acculturation of Aboriginal Australia as if the last two hundred years had been the creation of the "true" Australia. I want, therefore, to assert that if we must talk about "nature" and about the "raw materials" to be processed in the creation of a culture, then we must be prepared to say that any artifacts that exist in the environment are there to be acculturated. Artifacts such as glossy European art reproduction books, the promotional material of the several film industries vying for Australian dollars, the discourses of all the political regimes struggling for influence over the populace, the legends and characters from the multiple mythologies of the "outside world," the television programs that are available twenty-four hours per day—all this "stuff" might as well be regarded as "nature." It's what we work on to render the environment meaningful in our best interests.

Consider these two facts: (1) during millennia before the European incursion, Aboriginal society had turned the land of the Dreaming into an enormous sign; and (2) during centuries before the inauguration of white Australia, the South Land had already become a richly significant notion in European culture. These facts are now indisputable, and they mean that *any* culture operating in modern Australia has to be regarded as "low" because, within human memory, the country has never been pristine. Aesthetics in and of Australia must now incorporate the "unnatural" definitions of what gets counted as "raw material" for acculturation. Nature cannot be regarded as an apolitical entity waiting to be processed. Nature already *means* something.

The ramifications of such an adjustment are legion: mutations are required for ideas about imagination and creativity; pioneer history; rights of sovereignty and tenancy; property and copyright; subjectivity in relation to (rather than in contestation with) the environment. The list is exponential.

Accordingly, until an adjusted aesthetic is fully realized in Australia, a redefined landscape culture must be indecorous. Such a redefined culture must work on issues and elements that, according to "High Art" criteria, would be evaluated as "untouchable." The "new" landscape culture is "bad" art, therefore, inasmuch as it eschews traditional aesthetic classifications. It opts for reproducibility; it takes as its "issues" the images and themes that impinge on the broader populace; it interrogates traditional genres and tastes; it looks for beauty in change and adaptation rather than in originality and timelessness; it does not dismiss as "merely foreign" the forms and contents which have recently been imported from outside and which are becoming established and significant in local communities. It is "vulgar," therefore.

In orthodox terms, such a redefined landscape culture is "unnatural." In popular terms it is a site for contestation over what gets counted valuable in a community's cultural life. And, as in any postcolonial society, it is the popular cultures—the activities of communities at the domestic and vocational levels—which have meant that communities have persisted in Australia. The diary writers, storytellers, market gardeners, tunesmiths, list makers, "hobby" painters and quilters of the colonial era: they were engaged in a crucial culture, working daily to render the domestic sphere mundane (rather than "alien"), meaningful, *and* invigorating. Such artists have always galvanized and bound together a colonial community. And in contemporary white Australia, which is so evidently both a colonized and a colonizing entity, it is the vested interests of the popular arts (or more accurately the arts without tasteful hierarchy) that are still to be counted the most invigorating and humane. This is not an innocent assertion on my part: it is a question of where I take my pleasures and choose to invest my powers.

The notion of a communally invigorating (as opposed to divisive or exclusive) art seems intrinsic to the pictures in this essay. These works appear to mark a significant shift in the concerns of much photographically processed artwork in Australia. Unlike some of the more famous Australian photography of the 1960s and 1970s, these images are not singularly concerned to be "High Art." Nor are they deliberately "antiaesthetic," like much of the more influential work of the late 1970s. They are less anxious (some might say less "aggressive") to confront an audience, but they *are* asking that audience to think about change. While retaining an analytical (some might say "deconstructive") intent as they hold up a universe of forms and images to the judgment of the local community, they are also unabashed in their pursuit of aesthetic freshness, dynamism, or assurity (some might say "beauty"). This is syncretist work. But it is not necessarily promotional of a cozy national consensus. Rather, the artists find a community (for example, those people who know that their view of the world is negotiable and therefore mutable), and they serve that community.

And how does one "serve?" The myths, media, and formats that hold sway in any social group need to be interrogated, certainly, but just as surely it is now time to get on with the businesss of invigorating ourselves. It's time to stay true to the desiderata of a popular culture, which should help its several communities so that they can live as well as is possible and ethical. This is utopian, of course, but it's a utopianism with fewer illusions than modernism ever harbored about the individual's ability to transcend the tawdry concerns of the quotidian. This is sardonic utopianism, determinedly mundane yet ambitious to be celebratory; skeptical yet respectful of the values of the communities that administer it.

It is a culture that knows that there's no such thing as a purist position when dealing with notions like pleasure and power. It knows that a celebration can be neither simple nor innocent. And it knows that in a guilty pleasure, it's the pleasure that does the work, it's the pleasure that needs to be mobilized to work on the guilt, not the other way around. This is impure politics, of course, but I bet it's also popular politics.

Finally, I keep coming back to my dead American poets, and I read this snippet from Frank O'Hara:

I am ashamed of my century
for being so entertaining
but I have to smile.

And I reckon that, for now, such an admission might
not be a bad place to start again.

"Untitled No. 5," from the series *Debt,*
1987 (black and white photograph).
Jeff Gibson. Courtesy of the artist.

naar het Schilder - boeck

"Big Fish Eat Little Fish," from the series
Naar het Schilder-boeck, 1985 (silver
gelatin photograph, 110.5 × 109.2
cm). Jacky Redgate. Courtesy of the
Mori Gallery, Sydney.

"Chiswick 1953," from the series
photographer unknown, 1986 (silver
gelatin photograph, 76.2 × 50.6 cm).
Jacky Redgate. Courtesy of the Mori
Gallery, Sydney.

"Work-To-Rule IV," 1986/87
(cibachrome, 122 × 101 cm). Jacky
Redgate. Courtesy of the Mori
Gallery, Sydney.

"Eighty Million Eyes," from the series
Kiss Kiss Bang Bang, 1987
(cibachrome, 59.5 × 74.5 cm). Robyn
Stacey. Courtesy of the Mori-Gallery,
Sydney.

11

Paranoid Critical Methods

A Response to Peter Fuller's *The Australian Scapegoat: Towards an Antipodean Aesthetic**

The writer's resistance to nature . . . It lacks a
symbolic subtext, excepting that provided by man
. . . It inspires a painfully limited set of responses
in 'nature-writers'—REVERENCE, AWE, PIETY,
MYSTICAL ONENESS.

> Joyce Carol Oates, "Against Nature"

Peter Fuller's book on Australia, like most of his work,
pleads for an emphatic response from the reader. One senses
that he'd prefer the acclamation of agreement, but he'd settle
for controversy and disputation. *Anything,* rather than dis-
interest.

Given that I'm about to enter into dispute with *The Australian Scapegoat,* Fuller can probably count himself successful
yet again. I did consider the option of ignoring his strangely
archaic invocation of the spirit of imperialism. But the evidence

*University of Western Australia Press, 1986. In the interim between
my writing this chapter and its publication, Peter Fuller died, tra-
gically young. The man passed away but the author called Fuller prevails. His books are everywhere, exerting their influence. This chapter
is concerned with the author. For this reason I have chosen not to
alter the present tense in which the essay was originally drafted.

suggests that prejudices such as Fuller's won't go away unless they are chased. Moreover, in terms of polemical strategies, *The Australian Scapegoat* is an appropriate object around which to criticize Fuller's patrician attitudes and aesthetics. For Fuller has essayed a topic—i.e., Australia—which he understands less thoroughly than his audience does. He has slipped up quite badly this time, and it seems right and useful to call him to task now.

I want to start with an instance from recent North American culture. Almost certainly it's a moment that Fuller is not aware of. It's a scene from the David Cronenberg film, *Videodrome* (1983).

In this "monstrous" morality tale, James Woods plays an irresponsible grafter named Max. He runs a moderately successful, albeit legally dubious, TV station—Channel 21: "The station you go to bed with." The programs, of course, are softcore porn. Max is a purveyor of junk, but he knows it's a commodity with value (dollars, not ethics—Max is not an easy character to like) and with meaning, and he takes his work seriously. He's been looking to develop the station's repertoire, but in the previews he's been seeing nothing but "arty" stuff dressed up to connote the "Aesthetic" and the "Tasteful." Porn is what he deals in, and all he's getting is anachronisms that won't signal what they're really about; all he's getting is product made and hustled by people not prepared to admit that it's not "Taste" or "Art" they're dealing with.

Max has the intuition that something's changed, and Art—in the decorous, "elevating" sense of the word—is not a useful notion to bring to the world he's operating in. After yet another anticlimactic set of previews, in a moment of disdain that is both chilling and thrilling, Max stubs his cigarette into a grimy ashtray and declares that he's looking for "something . . . tough," he's looking for something "that'll break through." (Appropriately enough, he's in the market for a product that takes its concerns *to the max*.) He's grinding out a message in the butts and detritus: "Art" and "Taste" have to be radically redefined or else you might as well forget about them—unless you can convince yourself that the world hasn't changed in the last hundred years. If you can't acknowledge that junk culture exists and pervades, you'll never be able to fashion moments of significance from it. Nor will you understand the workings of your habitat. You will be unable to negotiate the world you live in. You will be looking for "Aesthetics" in a foreign place and a foreign time, fervidly trying to ignore the environment that people are now willingly acculturating.

Peter Fuller is almost certainly not aware of Max's quest. On the evidence of his published writing, particularly *The Australian Scapegoat*, Fuller would regard a film like Cronenberg's as tasteless, intellectually and aesthetically destitute, and ruinous to the individual and society. It is part of Fuller's project to abjure major portions of the cultural milieu in which art (regardless of how you define it) arises in the late-industrial West and in Australia particularly. He is simply ignorant of the nuances of much of the culture he avoids or condemns.

I am not referring to porn here, but to the cultures of communities that are prepared to criticize and humanize their environments. So I refer to cinema, photography, the mass media, popular music, many kinds of reading and writing, and the culture of selective consumption: all at the same time as I discuss art. But Fuller tries as much as possible to consider only "Art." And when you encounter such exclusive criticism, you have to ask how you could trust the analyses and the proclamations (the latter far outweigh the former in *The Australian Scapegoat*) presented by a writer who shows no inclination to redress his ignorance of the *gestalt* of which art (especially *Australian* art) partakes.

Now, given that I'm barely five hundred words into this chapter, it must seem indecorously early to be offering such a damning evaluation of *The Australian Scapegoat*. Protocol would require that I argue a few points with the author, tease out some discursive inconsistencies, and, finally, come to a gentlemanly assessment of the thoughts presented. But as Peter Fuller is well aware, protocol demands that I accept his project on his terms. Protocol dictates that when the author says the options of choice are A and B, I accept that those two variables are the ones to consider, I accept that the author is not willfully misrepresenting B, and I accept that the terms of debate are fair and equable. Protocol demands all that.

But this is not a fair or decorous book; not in the way it presents its nineteenth-century, Anglocentric view of world culture as natural and nonnegotiable even as it purports to espouse the virtues of localism; not in the rhetorical ploys its author uses to cosset himself and the reader in a chummy collectivity of references to "*our* world" and all the things the author informs "*us*" that "*we* need." (I'm reminded here of newspaper reports of a certain New South Wales politician's habit of slinging a matey arm over the shoulder of his interlocutor as he cajoles the victim into "seeing the practicalities.") So, indecorous as it is to say so, I'm making my position clear right away: this book is attempting to use and misrepresent *my* cultures (white Australian and multimedia) for its own benefit and I don't want any part of it; I don't trust this book; I don't like its assumptions and effects; and every time I feel that matey arm slip over my shoulder, I'm going to be vigilant, I'm going to try to figure out just how the book is maneuvering to put me where it wants me. Accordingly, my response is going to be an exercise in rhetoric at the same time as it will essay a few notions of culture, both colonial and contemporary.

Ironically, like Cronenberg's Max, Peter Fuller also professes to be looking for something that'll break through, some program that will lead out of what he perceives to be the dead end of late modernism. But Max and Fuller are looking in opposite directions, and although Max's world is far messier than the one Fuller yearns for, Cronenberg seems to me more culturally useful simply because he's better apprised of the circumstances in which people live and work *culturally* in contemporary late-industrial societies.

This is a great pity, for whenever *The Australian Scapegoat* promises, it also entices. For example, in addition to his intention to find a "path beyond the modernist impasse" [p. xiii], Fuller indicates that he is prepared to tackle the complex notion of the "aesthetic dimension" in art and work. When he defines cultural experience as the individual's "redemption from the insult of the Reality Principle" [p. 6], he would appear to be ready to elaborate a theory of cultural process in which the aesthetic and ethical qualities of a citizen's life are not neglected or undervalued in the larger political scheme, regardless of whether that scheme is designated capitalist or socialist.

Moreover, there is a refreshingly heretical character to the sources that Fuller cites as signposts on the path that he promises to survey. He mentions few of the texts that, by virtue of their very influence, are in danger of becoming thoughtlessly canonical in international art writing. Rather, he sketches out an intriguing configuration of Donald Winnicott, Sebastiano Timpanaro, John Ruskin, Herbert Marcuse, William Morris, and Rudolf Bahro. Feisty utopians, all.

So how is it that this Australian finds *The Australian*

Scapegoat so imperious? How is it that I find myself being used and abused by this book? Perhaps Ruskin's presence in the roll call is an early hint that Fuller's attitudes are not thoroughly egalitarian. But for me the dissimulation in the book becomes manifest when I concentrate on two motifs: firstly, Fuller's attitude to the *idea* of Australia and how it fits his schema of world influence, and, secondly, his anxiety when he finds himself lost in the complicated environment of the mass-mediated narratives and codes that so many people now choose to inhabit. As I will try to explain presently, in each case Fuller bases his opinion on a thoroughly conservative (*not* conservationist) understanding of the notion of "nature."

Take the manipulation of the idea of Australia. Consider the title: *The Australian Scapegoat: Towards an Antipodean Aesthetic*. The scapegoat reference makes it clear (with no deft sense of saving irony) that the image of Australia here is still a determinedly colonial one: Australia as the ritual bearer and purger of the traumas of a larger society elsewhere. If the imperial assumptions are not clear enough, the subtitle underlines them all. It is an *antipodean* aesthetic, not an Australian one, that the author is heading for. By definition, the orientation of an antipodean aesthetic must locate England as the principal reference point in the program. An antipodean aesthetic, then, must entail the deployment of the idea of Australia for the definitional purposes of an Anglocentric view of culture.

This reification of a colonial Australia occurs often in *The Australian Scapegoat*, but never with more panache than when the author offers a personal parable of consummation to explain the process by which he came to know the country. Following the title page, an epigraph is dedicated to a woman, addressed by her first name, "With love and thanks for turning my world upside down." Heartfelt enough, and apart from the dedication's reiteration of the antipodal placement of Australia relative to principal European experience, it would seem innocuous enough.

However, in Fuller's first chapter, entitled "Introduction: The Antipodes and I," this little overture is embellished. While describing his recognition of "the dreadful *otherness* of Australia" with its "second creation of strange" flora and fauna in "this intractable land" [p. xix], he insinuates an echoing theme. He explains how, in 1947 ("as it happens, the year in which I was born" [p. xvii]), Kenneth Clark visited Australia at a stage in his career when he was finalizing his *Landscape into Art*. On the boat bringing him out from England, Clark is supposed to have been compelled to "fight off the attentions of young women who wanted to interfere with this creative process" [p. xvii]. Clark tarried for no distraction and finished the draft. Fuller leaves the trysting in abeyance for the moment, simply making the point that Clark's book might have been different if he'd delayed finalizing it until he'd been exposed to the Australian environment.

A few pages later in the "Introduction," Fuller cuts in where Sir Kenneth had left off. Immediately after a paragraph of misinformed disparagement of traditional Aboriginal land culture, he tells his story of romance and marriage with the Australian woman mentioned in the book's epigraph. As this little myth of encounter is tied up, the traditional European relationship to Australia as other is also consummated. Australia is incorporated into a particular world schema as the "Introduction" comes to a close: "In this book, I argue that the image and symbol of nature which Australia proposes has a significance which extends far beyond the shores of the antipodes" [p. xxv].

If *The Australian Scapegoat* were intended to serve an

English readership, my objections might seem querulous. But despite Fuller's expressed hope that "Europeans may yet feel compelled, quite literally, to *look* to Australia" [p. xxv], the book is addressed directly to Australians, and it is imbued with a promethean aura of tutelage. (Twice in the "Acknowledgments" page, the author speaks of bringing the book to "the light of day.") And if the pupil accepts the hierarchy of pedagogy, if the pupil accepts the assignation of being pupil, there's no way to argue the position outside the prescriptions of authority. Better to reject the arrangement altogether; clearly, Fuller is not the only dealer with a possible local definition.

But just as clearly, he doesn't seem to know (or want to know) the alternatives. Rather, he is content to snuggle down in the warm affirmation of a solipsism based on the assumption that Europe is the source of greatness:

> There are important continuities between the best Australian landscape paintings of Sydney Nolan, Arthur Boyd, and Fred Williams, and the highest achievements of European art: indeed, these great Australian painters could not have achieved what they did if they had not steeped themselves in the great traditions of Western art. That is as things should be: the cultural roots of White Australia are European, and will always remain so [p. xxiv].

Fuller's deployment of such nonnegotiable "natural facts" is rhetorically duplicitous. Are there no other "great" Australian painters? Are there no other "great" traditions available? What is this singular white Australia which will always exist? This is a rhetoric which, by virtue of its specious simplicity, forecloses on possible discussions of multiplicity and complexity in the self, in the nation, in the real, or, indeed, in the natural.

Certainly Fuller's belief in certain natural facts is questionable. I could find plenty of people to gainsay his facts about his England "with its temperate climate, amenable to human life, and its richly fertile agricultural lands, regular, moderate and cyclical seasons" [p. 39]. These "facts" are relative and mutable, depending on the experiences one decides to call real or normal. Yemmerrawannie, the Aboriginal whom Arthur Phillip brought to England in 1792—and who quickly died in that new world—may well have challenged Fuller's facts about England. He probably also would have questioned "objective" renditions of Australia as "strange and intractable," "alien," inherently "deceitful," and redolent with a "dreadful *otherness*" [pp. xix–xxiv].

Fuller's rhetoric derives from his implicit belief in the irreducibility of the idea of nature. Let's return for a moment to the sentence in which he declares his intentions: "In this book, I argue that the image and symbol of nature which Australia proposes has a significance which extends far beyond the shores of the antipodes" [p. xxv]. This assertion is debatable almost to the point of being disingenuous. Australia proposes nothing at all. Images and symbols—semiotic entities with mutable meanings ascribed to them through social interaction—are proposed *for* Australia by intrepreters (English, Australian, or otherwise) who come to it with their own systems of meaning; the semiotic entities are proposed by interpreters who preselect the phenomena that are to be designated symbols. The question of whether or not there *is* some essential Australianness is a nonissue because, as soon as Australia means anything, it is meaning something precisely because it has been incorporated into the epistemology you profess. If Australia has some "true" character, it is not something that can be known outside of systems of perception and interpretation. Australia proposes nothing naturally. Australian propositions are social and political in their derivations and their dispositions.

The question I want to keep asking is, what does he want, the proposer portrayed in this book? One of the things he wants is to co-opt a colonial idea of Australia into his global scheme. If England and the world are to get well again, Australia will have to lend a hand. Something he does *not* want is to acknowledge that there is a sophisticated and motley populace that feels somehow at home here, and that it is not concerned to look to England for definition, affirmation, or purpose.

Something he *does* want is to convince his readers that, with some phenomena (and noumena), there is no other way—some things simply *are*. But let me resist this rhetorical feint with two ploys of my own. First, the quotation of an authoritative ally: as Joyce Carol Oates has said of the type of "nature-writing" she cannot abide, argument proceeds from a premise of "a Platonic, hence discredited, is-ness."[1] Second, a series of rhetorical questions: Australia proposes? Australia is? There are a few facts about Australia that you're going to have to face? It is common sense?

It is the kind of common sense, for example, that tries to persuade a reader not even to ponder the work assembled over decades of diligence in schools of phenomenological thought that are caricatured as "the theorists" [p. 14], "the Althusserians, Structuralists, Post-Structuralists, and what-have-you" [p. 46]. There is a rudimentary argumentative ploy in operation here. This is the gist of the tactic: you reduce a complex intellectual debate to a few deliberately inadequate and inaccurate labels, and then you leave it to common sense to suggest disregarding the entire rabble. It's the strawman maneuver—an old one, a tired one, but a distressingly effective one still, if it isn't pinpointed whenever it's used.

As Dana Polan has noted with reference to similar attempts to stifle a burgeoning sophistication in film criticism, "the seeming innocence of the appeal to common sense can so easily tie up with a whole disciplinary apparatus—humanism not as a defender of sense but as the forceful imposer of a particular sense."[2] The strategy of duplicitous name-calling has been a mainstay of Australian intellectual history, and it has invariably been used to validate a particular notion of "acceptable" writing, art, and culture. It's been well anatomized in books by John Docker and Tim Rowse.[3]

I'll describe the strategy quickly: an alarmist orthodoxy (say, a traditionally influential University Department of English), with a publishing facility and access to other avenues of debate or instruction, perceives a threat mustering up from the left. Through all its dissemination channels the Department begins to characterize itself as a victim, loudly proclaiming itself to be constantly drowned out by some bullying, all-powerful but unnamed (or caricatured) "tendency" or unruly mob. With such a gesture to this ill-described, partially imagined specter, the Department harnesses the paranoia of the conservative factions of cultural administration, and a campaign is mounted to liberate the embattled custodians of plain speaking and common sense. A move to the right is a move to freedom and fair dealing.

This intellectual gerrymander is also a time-honored ploy

in Australian journalism. And in the local context, Fuller's deliberately alarmist book fits with designed exactitude into the apparatus of censure.

So, according to Fuller's paranoid critical method, "the theorists" are out to obfuscate a few plain truths, and he's a voice in the wilderness calling for a return to the "true antipodean aesthetic" [p. xxv] as purveyed by early Boyd and Nolan and late Williams. "It seemed to me," the author professes levelheadedly, "that Nolan, Boyd, and in a rather different and special way, Fred Williams, had all begun to propose a new aesthetic, involving a new vision of the natural world, and man's place within it" [p. xxi].

Truthful, visionary art like Williams's Pilbara paintings! The Pilbara as region of spiritual transcendence where the greatest heroism, the greatest humanity, must come from the mining companies that could tame such a place and leave it better than they found it! How many times must this *trompe l'oeil* be pointed out? I suppose as often as someone with access to a widespread audience *refuses* to point it out. Really, how "new" and how elevating is this vision?

The characterization of the great artist as someone who can rescue "us" from some contemporary blight or lead "us" out of a cultural desert is crucial to Fuller's argumentative protocol. The commonsense premise is that the world, "our" world, is in a state of crisis and that the task of the critic is to discern which artists are "our" saviors, which artists make paintings that will enable "us" to evolve out of the recidivist "tendencies" [p. 49] that afflict "us," and which artists are holding "us" down in the mire. Protocol would demand that the reader engage in this severely circumscribed debate.

But the terms of debate are negotiable. The notion of

crisis is a moot one, as is the status of nature as the ideal by which to assess truth and regain "our" sense of universal orientation. If Fuller's aesthetic is radical, it is radically regressive in its advocacy of a *return* to nature rather than a *redefinition* of what is nature nowadays. He opts for an antique Platonism which defines nature as a given rather than as a cultural construct; nature as ideal rather than as mediated idea.[4]

What I want to resist is the effect, not so much the antiquity, of the Platonism. For the idealism engenders a patrician attitude toward all mediated discourses, all discourses that are expressed through mechanisms other than the human hand, discourses by which a great many people choose to think and know and feel. Of course, such valorization of the chirographic arts also operates on the dubious assumption that they are not mediated (as if the body were not already *constructed* socially as well as "naturally") and are thus directly connected to a sphere of natural or ideal significance. But more pertinently, in terms of the *effects* of Fuller's idealism, his arbitration necessarily defines and condemns second and third degree representation as unnatural and obfuscatory.

If this term "nature" must be deployed, I would like to clarify what it means to whomever is deploying it. If it is related somehow to a notion of the given environment that one is born into and that one must work and play upon (or acculturate) in order to humanize one's existence, then I'm prepared to claim as part of my nature not only sunshine, clouds, landforms, and all things "green," but also the cinema, television, pop music, books, motor cars, magazines, and all available mass-mediated images and sounds. All this nature is part of my culture. Such is the environment I perceive and accept

as a natural (though mutable) fact. I'm even prepared to celebrate aspects of it, to ascribe meaning to portions of it, to
work to conserve elements of it.

I'm prepared to say that it is necessary to redefine the
notion of nature because there has been a fundamental (and
not necessarily invidious) change to the human environment
as I understand and inhabit it. To return to the example of
Cronenberg's *Videodrome*, one can argue, as the film does in
its own melodramatic way, that the space and time that a great
many people now inhabit are crucially (which is not to say
exclusively) connected to the mass media, and that, for these
people, this is now a "natural" fact that will never be reversed.
Indeed, as the film also implies, this twentieth-century ontolog-
ical shift has meant that the limits of the body, of individual
consciousnesses, and of nervous systems all ought to be re-
drawn. Moreover there is no plausible reason to bemoan this
fact—no more than there is reason for bemoaning the fact
that the sun is in the sky. People know about the media as
an aspect of their environment and they use them as they see
fit. It then becomes a question of *how* people use the elements
of that newly defined environment, just as people have traditionally used the sun and sea while knowing how to avoid
the perceptible dangers.

Do the people who inhabit and administer such an environment deserve to be told they are "recidivist" or "degener-
ate?" Do they deserve such censure particularly if they are consciously attempting to conserve the evidently invigorating
aspects of that environment at the same time as they attempt
to delimit what they perceive, from their own intimate knowledge of their milieu, to be pollutant in their locality?

In response to such queries it's not too fanciful to talk
of a postmodernist, second-degree kind of cultural ecology,

provided you've already arrived at a redefinition of "nature" in this time and place. It's not too fanciful, then, to consider Juan Davila's paintings, for example, as an attempt to elaborate an ecology out of the complexities of the popular cultural environment of Australia—with its pollution and its exhilaration, with all its nationalism, internationalism, and colonialism.

Once you've redefined "nature," or maybe "landscape," as Fuller refuses to do, you can actually agree with much of his polemic. For example, I wouldn't want to resist his call for a concentration of artistic energies on "the local landscapes that are most peoples' experiences of nature, and . . . [on] the variety of personal meanings which they hold for us" [p. 38]. Nor could I argue with his proclamation that "we need to evolve an aesthetic rooted in the imaginative response to nature, to the whole world of natural form" [p. 50].

Once you've redefined "nature," or maybe "environment," you can come to a more viable comprehension of "the local." You might start to understand how the definition of location in Australia must nowadays take heed of the effects of transnational media, shifting spheres of geopolitical influence, and the epistemological changes brought about in citizens as a result of their increased mobility within systems of communication and information. A notion of locality can entail all these things, without negating the continuing influence of more traditional criteria of place: longitude, latitude, climate, longrunning legends, myths, histories, and economic dependencies. That's how big it is, the "whole world of natural form."

But I'm enacting a process of redefinition that Fuller refuses to countenance. Basic to his aesthetic is an assumption derived from Timpanaro: "Since the beginning of civilisation, men and women have lived their lives in bodies which are

very much as they are now" [p. 50]. This assertion is presented
as another natural fact. But it precludes any discussion of the
changes that have occurred in the ways people have deployed
their bodies through the agency of technology. Timpanaro's
line of argument is meant to justify Fuller's exclusive interest
in the chirographic arts, as he elaborates: "Despite advances
in technology, the capacity and potentiality of the human hand
in relation to stone, and other materials, has not changed
greatly since Sumerian times" [p. 53]. This may well be true,
but it is no reason to ignore the changes that *have* occurred
in peoples' relationships to their environments and their com-
municative media. It is a *non sequitur* (even if one holds firm
to a belief in a Platonic "is-ness") to infer that art has not
developed in media processed by devices other than the hand.

Fuller builds his aesthetic on a misunderstanding of the
culture of participatory consumption, something he mis-
recognizes as "spectacle": "Spectacle is something imposed
on people, or piped onto them: they receive it passively, and
they do not participate, affectively, physically or culturally in
its creation. Advertising, of course, is cynically produced: no
one believes that using one brand of detergent rather than
another actually deepens family love" [p. 57].

Of course advertising is cynically produced! Consumers
know that! Hasn't Fuller looked closely at advertising lately?
The outsider's stance he takes on what he calls the spectacle
indicates that he does not understand this culture internally
or (dare I say it) structurally. Moreover, it's a slovenly discursive ploy to conflate mediatized culture with advertising, especially when one's understanding of the rhetorics of persuasion
evince no intimate understanding of the timbres of irony and
skepticism that suffuse the promotion of commodity-culture.

Evidently Fuller is not a regular tiller in the fertile fields of mediatized popular culture. (I invoke the connotations of "natural" fecundity advisedly.) He doesn't understand the active and adaptive ingenuity which consumers bring to that culture. He refuses to acknowledge that this knowingness is something to celebrate, something a good deal more laudable than the feigned innocence subtending the presumption that Art (Italian Renaissance painting, for example, or even William Morris's prodigious humanitarian output) is not produced for the mundane purposes of political persuasion and the imposition of a particular sense.

Moreover, Fuller appears unaware that the culture of participatory consumption has histories, traditions, scholars, and unremittingly creative artists. It comes down to a substantive issue: if he can't see it, he can't see it. But I can only avow that there are many who can see it, and I ask what right he has to deny those people their sight. By way of clinching his argument, Fuller declaims that "good art can only be realised when a creative individual encounters a living tradition with deep tendrils in communal life" [p. 15]. By way of clinching *my* argument I'd like to use the same quote. Surely, to indulge some of my own peccadilloes, a rock album as grand as Ed Kuepper's *Electrical Storm*, or a photographic work as enduring and evocative as Jacky Redgate's series from the past ten years, or a text as caustically vitalist as Mark Thirkell's "Satire: An Essay on Form"[5] (all of which would be classified "not art" by Fuller) has developed out of encounters with living traditions operative in vibrant communal networks. Broadly speaking, it's a question of redefining one's idea of art. But more particularly, it's a matter of whether one has the mental suppleness to redefine one's notion of community.

It is Fuller's intransigence, finally, that makes *The Australian Scapegoat* so frustrating. Even when I can agree with some of the general aesthetic contentions, I'm compelled to dispute their specific application. For example, when Fuller calls for an art that would "celebrate the value of an informed provincial vision, and of conservationist aesthetics" [p. xxiv], I can't help but feel that if he were better informed of the intricacies of location and environment which color the work of artists like Juan Davila or Mike Parr (two of Fuller's *bêtes noires* in the book), he would understand that, with his own words, he has defined rather than defamed their practices.

His condemnation of Davila is anxious indeed. One can only speculate about the reasons for the stridency of judgment. (Fuller refuses to engage in any specific analysis of the paintings themselves, adjudging them, along with Parr's work, to be "simply too unpleasant to describe in any detail" [p. 27].) I suggest that the refusal to examine the issues and the import of work such as Davila's in the context of Australian art and politics is somehow connected with the way these paintings disallow the possibility of returning Australia to the nineteenth-century world of Anglican propriety, stable humanist subjectivity, and pure, natural referentiality that Fuller would like to inhabit. It's not criticism he's up to here, but police work enforcing a clampdown on difference.

There can be no fruitful *rapprochement* between a critic like Fuller and art that does not engage in the values of the Anglocentric humanist. There are two incommensurable discourses operating. In the final analysis it comes down to admitting this, and leaving it at that. It is politic, at last, to refuse to engage in Fuller's rhetoric. His discourse is persuasive precisely because it seems so commonsensical, precisely because it doesn't display its mechanisms of coercion for what they effectively are. It is for this reason that I have taken a long road to find the right word in response to *The Australian Scapegoat*. The word? To speak plainly: NO!

"GULF," 1983 (oil on canvas, 274 ×
274 cm). Juan Davila. Courtesy of the
Roslyn Oxley Gallery, Sydney.

12

The Body on the Bed

In Sydney, if you pick your time judiciously—say, Wednesday, 9:45 AM, after peak hour and just before the commercial delivery vehicles have left the warehouses—you can drive from St. Ives to St. Peters, north to south, in just under an hour. It's a short pilgrimage that can jeopardize your sense of who and where you are.

St. Ives is probably a good place to put behind you first thing in the morning. Over the last few years, some of the estate agents who deal in the blue ribbon properties of the area have taken to subtitling their sales notices in Afrikaans, and the citizens of less "grand-and-green" suburbs have renamed the place "St. Africa." Elsewhere in the world, something is happening, and Krugerands are having a definite though discreet impact right here.

So, it's 9:45 AM, and you drive past the auction rooms and head out on to the Pacific Highway, main artery to the heartland of Liberal-voting middle-Australia: Pymble, Gordon, Lindfield, Roseville, Chatswood, Gore Hill; through enclaves in St. Leonards and Crow's Nest where estate agents and smallgoods shops are festooned with Japanese characters. Fifteen more minutes take you through North Sydney, across the Harbour Bridge and into the Central Business District, all serviced by multinational capital, especially American and Japanese, (although Hong Kong money is also buying up big now that the lease on the "British" island is truly running out). Trundle in second gear south of the CBD: On to George Street, past the Hollywood moviehouses of Hoyts and Greater Union, across the Spanish strip of southern Liverpool Street and through a large and expanding Chinatown. On to Broadway: three sets of lights, and the road forking right leads up to Leichhardt and Sydney's largest Italian community. But the road bending left is the one you take, past the cloistered and quadrangled University; into Newtown—traditionally Greek, Lebanese, and Anglo-Saxon proletarian, but more recently under the newer influences of three-tiered Vietnamese families and yuppie refurbishing. Three gears and four sets of lights take you down Newtown's fabled King Street: roads to the left lead to Alexandria, Erskineville, and to Redfern, where the most visible people, the people who define the place, are Koori. South out of Newtown, finally, and on to the Princes Highway, which is idling with two generic car types—the remodeled Datsuns and Toyotas currently popular among Austro-Vietnamese youth, and the 1970s Holdens and Falcons seemingly preferred by the Melanesians who have moved into St. Peters over the last decade. Falcons are parked outside Fijian supermarkets run principally by Indian retailers. Purple Datsuns stud the clearways beside the clothing and laundry sweatshops that operate behind the blanked-out windows of rented properties which used to house Cypriot record shops and "Australian and Continental" bakeries.

Drive for sixty minutes in any direction in Sydney, and you cross communities that will respond with indifference to Anglo-Australian cricket matches, Bicentennial celebrations, or Federal elections. Indeed, from many points of view, the only encouraging aspect of the proliferation of nationalist ceremonies throughout the 1980s was the possibility that, in attempting to rerun and refine its myths of unification and authorization, white middle-class Australia presented itself to public scrutiny at a time when it was demonstrably no longer in charge of the vital or constituent factors of a future Australian society. There is a chance that in the years to come, for every celebratory national event that is stage-managed, only a fraction of the populace will count themselves included.

Stick a pin in any sector of the map, and polyglot communities can be located, from Broome to Burnie to Barcaldine. (When I rang SBS—the nationwide, "multicultural" broadcaster—to ascertain how many language groups they served Australiawide, they could not give an exact number, but guessed it to be in excess of seventy-five.) If there must be festivals of nationhood, the best thing to celebrate thereby is the fact that a nation is not a natural thing and that it is therefore subject to change and redefinition. On a world scale this is obvious. The history of warfare is the history of nations undergoing or resisting transmogrification at the behest of social (not natural) forces. Or to state the same case in slightly different discursive terms, until recently the history of global economics has been the history of waxing and waning national entities.

In my limited vocation as a cultural critic, therefore, I tend to seize enthusiastically on "aberrant" works of "Australian" art in order to emphasize the volatility of national definitions and discourses. Hence it is for modest reasons of destabilization that I choose to write about Geoff Weary's short super-8 film, *Venezuela*.

If forums are still being convened nowadays to discuss the nation, I am happiest to be involved in any project that disturbs the relationship of a citizen to a fatherland. For, once that disturbance has occurred, reconciliation is set in play, and it is in this Oedipal kind of ceremony that mutation and surprise are possible. (I am taking it for granted that we are in agreement, you and I, that we are desirous of change.)

Venezuela is a difficult object to represent in any form other than its original. Would that I could simply show you the film. It is the perennial quandary for the cineaste: how (or, indeed, *whether*) to describe a film in the medium of the printed word. In the case of *Venezuela*, particularly, the object keeps changing purposefully in front of one's eyes and ears, and words can only *evoke* rather than *render* that evanescence. Would that I could simply show you the film. Would that I could be confident that you will one day see the film. But in the complex of financing, investment, and public taste that governs the possibilities of a film culture in a client-state like Australia, *Venezuela* is the kind of product that can be most influential through the bush telegraph of criticism, word-of-mouth—through redescription in other words.

In *Venezuela*, static, black and white images of a handsome man and a beautiful woman ooze throughout the film's duration. The characters are framed alone and distracted, but they are edited so that they occupy the same narrative (and possibly the same domestic) space. The characters adopt their ambiguous poses, which could connote joy, abandon, lassitude, or distress, depending on how the contextual details accumulate through time. Meanwhile the soundtrack is coming from several different directions. A male voice talks in English about the geographical, economic, and meteorological characteristics of Venezuela. A Spanish man replicates the information in his vernacular. A dance band plays stereotypical Latino *canciones* celebrating the carefree life. Elsewhere, but close at hand, on the soundtrack, jet engines shriek overhead.

All the while, the images of the supine protagonists continue their implied dalliance, brought together as they are, shot to shot, on the editing bench.

Venezuela enacts repeated dramas of encounter. How to describe, for example, any relationship between a woman and a man? Or, what of the bond between a citizen and a state? These private dramas on these beds, within these rooms, how can they be related to the world outside, where bands play for strangers and jet engines howl for conflict? How to graft all the details into a larger coherence, a bigger story?

As I see and hear it, *Venezuela* sets up a minimalist analysis of the dynamics between people and their environments at personal, communal, and national levels. In fact, on reflection (and reflection is what *Venezuela* demands of you) I would be hesitant to call it an analytic work. Perhaps it is more accurately described as catalytic. It is a collection of cues priming a kind of ruminative investigation. By supplying the barest details of several interconnecting stories concerning encounter and conciliation, it calls forth a "bardic" impulse in its audience. The stories are there: they are your stories if you want them; now you must exercise your right to tell (or to disbe-lieve). It is a right that can ail if not excercised. It is the right to have a say in what gets counted true.

There are at least three functions you can perform when participating in *Venezuela*: first you can recognize the details for all their potential meanings; next you can select some de-tails and piece them together into a particular myth (or narra-tive); and finally you can decide how to interweave the several myths into a mythology, something multidimensional that is undeniably fictional but also undoubtedly constitutive of what is called true in a community or even in a nation.

When I ponder each detail of *Venezuela* I see and hear the simplest elements of cinema: a few still images conjoined; some sounds overlayed. Each image is carefully chosen and precisely framed; the same may be said of each sound. In fact, this action of framing—a definitive factor of cinema—is ex-plicit throughout the entire work, both in the imagery and on the soundtrack. All the aural discourses—the geographi-cal empiricism, the economic account of the state of the na-tion, the bilingual cajolery on the commentary, the kitsch "SouthAmericana" of the music—they are all modes by which the profusion of possible meanings can be restricted; they are framing devices delimiting the connotations of the perceptible world so that *something* can be understood.

Because framing wrenches things from their *gestalt*, it enacts deception even as it enables perception. So, to realign the lie on which truth is inevitably constructed, one needs to recombine the details as soon as they are perceived. This collo-cation, of course, is the other crucial operation in cinema: the alchemical process of montage, the creation of a third meaning from the encounter of two preexistent elements.

So, just as framing is a cardinal concern in *Venezuela* so

the dynamics of *conjunction* are also vital. Everything in this piece makes sense (to quote the soundtrack) "only in a relative sense": the liberality of Venezuela; a woman alone in a room and a man alone in a room; the economic interdependencies of the South American dominions as they establish accords to compete against "first-world" capital; the paradisaic qualities of regions defined as exotic by the leisure-seeking West. Such details must be connected if meaning is to arise in *Venezuela*. One must then reflect more intently, and ask *which connections* and *which meanings* have been orchestrated by the text.

These are the motivating questions in *Venezuela*. Take a woman's body on a bed; take a man's body on a bed: what do they mean? I can only look to the context in which I find the images. I look and listen closely, but, as some notions are clarified, the film also remains determinedly ambiguous. Perhaps it is true to say that by refusing to be unequivocal about the definitive characteristics of Venezuela and these peoples' roles inside that *polis* as it is represented, the film is determinedly realistic. Take these people on these beds. As the details surrounding the bodies change, so the bodies change, just as a nation must alter in concert with adjustments to its international context.

Initially, the woman is "foreign" and "alone," as the soundtrack informs. As her image is montaged with other information, both visual and aural, she becomes not only a particular woman with a specific story, but also several generic Women. At one moment when the soundtrack murmurs, "Como está, Senorita?" she is the generalized object of Machismo romance. At other times, she is represented as the stereotypical object of a male photographer's libidinous aesthetic. And on occasions throughout the film, she appears also to be South America "herself," as the explicitly cliched signs and details of allure, "paradis," and natural abundance accrete to her while the narrative proceeds. Is it distress or happiness that I can read on her face?

As for the man, initially, he is dead and violated. This reading arises because his image appears amidst a trace of violence and repression that lurks in the image-series. A few frames beforehand, a man and a woman have encountered each other, surprisingly, in a single image, and someone else, someone behind the man, has been responsible for the welts I can see on his back. When the male body next appears on the bed, therefore, it takes on the squalid aura of the torture photos that seem generically South American. However, later on, the same corpse appears on the same bed, and the holiday music is playing. Suddenly it comes alive as a rich man's body, relaxed and smug in an exotic playground.

Is the image any less violent now that it has changed? Moreover, is the image any less true than it was in its original appearance?

Venezuela is a romance. But what kind of romance? It is an attempt to dramatize the very notion of *encounter*. A woman meets a country; a man meets a woman; an image meets an image; a sound meets a sound; an image meets a sound; a country meets a country. Depending on how these encounters are negotiated the romance will be more or less a story of colonization. Whose system of meaning will prevail? That is a question that bears down on everyone participating in the romance.

Recently I reread a brochure from one of the "historical entertainments" at World Expo '88 in Brisbane. It spoke of "the romance of our past." Paradoxically, it convinced me that it is right to describe Weary's minimalist Latino lyric as inherently Australian.

Notes

1. The Middle Distance

1. Walter J. Ong, "System, Space and Intellect in Renaissance Symbolism," in his *The Barbarian Within, and Other Fugitive
Essays and Studies* (New York: Macmillan, 1962), pp. 69–70. See
also Ong's *Interfaces of the Word: Studies in the Evolution of Consciousness and Culture* (Ithaca: Cornell, 1977) for an account of
the evolution of a "spatial" consciousness directly related to the
gradual refinement of "reflexive" disciplines such as poetics and
aesthetics in European culture.

2. Ong, "System, Space and Intellect," p. 75.

3. Ong, p. 76.

4. At the same time as subjective relations to environment
were undergoing such fundamental change, concomitant developments were occurring in the distribution and production of wealth

in Europe, as peasant and artisanal economies were being superseded by inchoate models of industrial capitalism. It is probably pointless to ponder which sea change came first—the epistemological or the economic—but the similarities in the symptoms of change are striking when we compare the history of European ideas with the history of European economics as described by Pierre Clastres:

> What is it about Western civilisation that makes it infinitely more ethnocidal than all the other forms of society? It is its *system of economic production*, which is precisely a space of the unlimited, a space without places, since it is in constant retreat from limits, an infinite space in permanent forward flight. What differentiates the West is capitalism, as much in the impossibility of remaining on this side of a frontier as in passing beyond every frontier [Pierre Clastres, "On Ethnocide," *Art & Text* 28 (March 1988), p. 57].

5. B. A. Upsenky, "'Left' and 'Right' in Icon Painting," *Semiotica* 13 (1975), pp. 33–39.

6. David Collins, *An Account of the English Colony in New South Wales* (London: Cadell & Davies, 1798), pp. 5–6.

7. Robert Kenny, "A Secret Australia," epilogue essay in Ken Taylor, *A Secret Australia* (Melbourne: Rigmarole, 1984), p. 88.

8. See, for example: Leo Marx, *The Machine in the Garden: Technology and the Pastoral Ideal in America* (New York: Oxford University Press, 1976); Hugh Honour, *The New Golden Land: European Images of America from the Discoveries to the Present Time* (London: Allen Lane, 1976); Henri Baudet, *Paradise on Earth: Some Thoughts on European Images of Non-European Man* (New Haven: Yale University Press, 1965); Harry Levin, *The Myth of the Golden Age in the Renaissance* (New York: Oxford University Press, 1969).

9. Burton Pike, *The Image of the City in Modern Literature* (Princeton: Princeton University Press, 1981), p. 25.

10. Thomas Mitchell, *Three Expeditions into the Interior of*

Eastern Australia, 2 vols. (London: T. & W. Boone, 1838), vol. 1, p. 5.

11. Mitchell, *Three Expeditions*, vol. 2, p. 170.

12. Charles Sturt, *A Narrative of an Expedition into Central Australia*, 2 vols. (London: T. & W. Boone, 1849), vol. 2, p. 2.

13. Kenny, "A Secret Australia," pp. 92–93.

2. Letters from Far-Off Lands

1. First editions of *Letters from an Exile* . . . (Penrith: Ann Bell, n.d.) are virtually nonexistent as far as the general public is concerned. One copy exists in the Mitchell Library, Sydney, and one is in the British Library. In 1945 George Mackaness privately published one hundred copies of the book, few of which survive outside major metropolitan libraries in Australia. Then, in 1979, Review Publications Pty. Ltd., of Dubbo, NSW, reprinted Mackaness's edition in an unnumbered, but undoubtedly limited, printing. Bernard Smith presented selected excerpts of the original in his *Documents on Art and Taste in Australia: The Colonial Period, 1770–1914* (Melbourne: Oxford University Press, 1975). An unabridged edition of the *Letters* is now widely available: Paul Foss, ed., *Island in the Stream* (Sydney: Pluto Press, 1988). All references to *Letters* are taken from the Foss (1988) edition.

2. The best account of Watling's background occurs in : Hugh Gladstone, *Thomas Watling, Limner of Dumfries* (Dumfries: privately published, 1938).

3. Certificate of the Sheriff Substitute of Dumfries, June 4th, 1789, quoted in George Mackaness, ed., "Introduction" to *Letters from an Exile* (Sydney: privately published, 1945), p. 6.

4. Letter from the Lord Advocate, Hay Campbell, to Evan Nepean, Under Secretary of the Home Office and Secretary to the Admiralty; quoted in Mackaness's "Introduction," p. 9.

5. Hay Campbell to Evan Nepean, quoted in Mackaness's "Introduction," p. 9.

6. See Gillian Beer, "'The Face of Nature': Anthropomorphic Elements in the Language of *The Origin of the Species,*" in L. J. Jordanova, ed., *Languages of Nature: Critical Essays on Science and Literature* (London: Free Association Books, 1986), pp. 212–43.

7. James Smith, *A Specimen of the Botany of New Holland* (1793), quoted in Bernard Smith, *European Vision and the South Pacific*, 2nd ed. (Sydney: Harper and Row, 1985), p. 5.

8. Hence one of the problems of Bernard Smith's anthologizing only the explicitly aesthetic tracts of *Letters* when he published excerpts in his *Documents on Art and Taste in Australia*. Although Smith affirms in *European Vision and the South Pacific* that *Letters* is an important document in the history of ideas concerning Australian nature, the exigencies of anthology publication meant that the full complexity of *Letters* went unrepresented in the *Documents*.

9. Paul Ricoeur, *The Rule of Metaphor: Multidisciplinary Studies in the Creation of Meaning in Language* (London: Routledge and Kegan Paul, 1978), p. 22.

10. Ricoeur, *The Rule of Metaphor*, p. 99.

11. Pierre Fontanier, *Les Figures du discours* (1830), quoted in Ricoeur, *The Rule of Metaphor*, p. 56.

12. Patricia S. Yaeger, "Coleridge, Derrida, and the Anguish of Writing," *SubStance* 39 (1983), p. 91.

13. Yaeger, "Coleridge, Derrida, and the Anguish of Writing," p. 91.

14. Smith, *European Vision and the South Pacific,* p. viii.

15. Jacques Lacan, "The Function and Field of Speech and Language in Psychoanalysis," in *Ecrits* (London: Tavistock, 1977), p. 70.

16. Peter Brooks, *The Melodramatic Imagination: Balzac, Henry James, Melodrama, and the Mode of Excess* (New Haven: Yale University Press, 1976), p. 67.

17. In Marker's films *Letter from Siberia, Sunday in Peking, Description of Combat, Cuba Si, Sunless,* and *La Jetée,* respectively.

3. The Nature of a Nation

1. Marcus Clarke, "Preface," *The Poems of the Late Adam Lindsay Gordon* (London: Samuel Mullen, 1887), pp. v–vi.

2. G. F. W. Hegel, in E. F. Carritt, ed., *Philosophies of Beauty* (Oxford: Clarendon Press, 1931), pp. 161–62.

3. Guiseppe de Santis, "Towards an Australian Landscape," in David Overbey, ed., *Springtime in Italy: A Reader on Neo-Realism* (London: Talisman, 1978), p. 125.

4. John Hinde, *Other People's Pictures* (Sydney: ABC, 1980).

5. Sergei Eisenstein, *Film Form: Essays in Film Theory,* edited and translated by Jay Leyda (New York: Harvest, 1949), p. 46.

6. I am indebted here to Meaghan Morris's article on *Crocodile Dundee:* "Tooth and Claw: Tales of Survival and *Crocodile Dundee,*" *Art & Text* 25 (June–August 1987), pp. 36–69.

4. Geography and Gender

1. Jacques Derrida, *Of Grammatology*, translated by G. C. Spivak (Baltimore: Johns Hopkins University Press, 1976), p. 127.

2. Paul Virilio, "Moving Girl," *Semiotext(e) Polysexuality* 4 (1981), pp. 242–48. All references to Virilio in this chapter are derived from this source.

3. Ferdinando de Oviedo, "Of Venomous Apples" (ca. 1600), in Samual Purchas, ed., *Hakluytus Posthumus* (Glasgow: Maclehose, 1905), vol. 15, p. 191.

4. Virilio, "Moving Girl," p. 243.

5. David Collins, *An Account of the English Colony in New South Wales* (London: Cadell & Davies, 1798), p. 6.

6. Thomas Mitchell, *Three Expeditions into the Interior of Eastern Australia* (London: T. & W. Boone, 1838), vol. 2, p. 170.

7. Charles Sturt, *Two Expeditions into the Interior of Southern*

Australia (London: Smith, Elder and Co., 1833), vol. 1, p. 157.

8. Charles Sturt, *Narrative of an Expedition into Central Australia* (London: T. & W. Boone, 1849), vol. 2, p. 2.

9. Sturt, *Two Expeditions*, vol. 2, p. 162.

5. Beyond the Compass of Words

1. *The Narrative of Arthur Gordon Pym* (1837) and "A Descent into the Maelstrom" (1841) are the other two maritime stories.

2. On more than one occasion Poe recorded his admiration for Defoe and Swift. See for example his review of *Robinson Crusoe* in the *Southern Literary Magazine*, Jan. 1836. See also B. R. Pollin, "Dean Swift in the Works of Poe," *Notes and Queries* 20 (1973), pp. 244–46.

3. See R. L. Rhea, "Some Observations on Poe's Origins," *Texas Studies in English* 10 (1930), pp. 135–46. See also, J. O. Bailey, "Sources for Poe's *Arthur Gordon Pym,* 'Hans Pfall' and Other Pieces," *PMLA* 57 (1942), pp. 513–35.

4. E. A. Poe, "A MS. Found in a Bottle," *Selected Writings of Edgar Allan Poe,* ed. David Galloway (Harmondsworth: Penguin, 1967), p. 99. All future references to "MS." will be to this edition and will be cited parenthetically in the text.

5. Ernst Cassirer, *The Philosophy of Symbolic Forms,* vol. 2: *Mythical Thought* (New Haven: Yale University Press, 1955), p. 5.

6. Bob Hawke, A.L.P. Policy Speech, 16 February 1983, Sydney Opera House; printed in *National Reconciliation: The Speeches of Bob Hawke, Prime Minister of Australia,* selected by John Cook (Sydney: Fontana/Collins, 1984), pp. 11–12.

7. E. A. Poe, "Between Wakefulness and Sleep," from "Marginalia," in *The Unknown Poe: An Anthology of Fugitive Writings by Edgar Allan Poe,* edited by Raymond Foye (San Francisco: City Lights, 1980), p. 42.

8. See Peter Brooks, *The Melodramatic Imagination: Balzac,*

Henry James, Melodrama and the Mode of Excess (New Haven: Yale University Press, 1976), pp. 72–73.

9. Donald Stauffer, "The Two Styles of Poe's 'MS. Found in a Bottle,'" *Style* 1 (1967), p. 108.

10. Stanley Cavell, "In Quest of the Ordinary: Texts of Recovery," in Morris Eaves and Michael Fischer, eds., *Romanticism and Contemporary Criticism* (Ithaca: Cornell University Press, 1986), p. 190.

11. Charles Baudelaire, in *The Unknown Poe*, p. 86.

6. The Keen Historic Spasm

1. James Agee and Walker Evans, *Let Us Now Praise Famous Men* (1941; rpt. London: Picador, 1988), pp. 38–39.

2. John Collier, Jr., "Photography and Visual Anthropology," in Paul Hockings, ed., *Principles of Visual Anthropology* (The Hague: Mouton, 1975), pp. 211–12.

3. Collier, "Photography and Visual Anthropology," p. 213.

4. James Clifford, "On Ethnographic Authority," in *The Predicament of Culture: Twentieth-Century Ethnography, Literature and Art* (Cambridge, Mass.: Harvard University Press, 1988). See also David Bennett, "Cultural Heritage and the Archive: Identity as Property," *Photofile* (Autumn 1989), pp. 18–21, and Alan Sekula, "The Body and the Archive," *October* 39 (Winter 1986), pp. 3–64.

5. A. Kibedi Varga, "Stories Told by Pictures," *Style* 22, no. 2 (Summer 1988), p. 196.

6. Nicholas Peterson, "The Popular Image," in Ian Donaldson and Tamsin Donaldson, eds., *Seeing the First Australians* (Sydney: George Allen and Unwin, 1985), pp. 164–65.

7. City Group, "Deconstruction in Camera: THOMAS ANDREW," *Photofile* (Spring 1988), p. 31.

8. Jean-François Lyotard, "Answering the Question: What

Is the Post-Modern?" *Zx: A Magazine of the Visual Arts* (Sydney) (Winter 1984), p. 12.

    9. Derrick Price, "Photographing the Poor and the Working Classes," *Framework* 22/23 (Autumn 1983), p. 21.

    10. James Engell, *The Creative Imagination: Enlightenment to Romanticism* (Cambridge, Mass.: Harvard University Press, 1981), p. 237.

    11. Agee and Evans, *Let Us Now Praise Famous Men,* p. 238.

    12. Walter J. Ong, *Orality and Literacy: The Technologising of the Word* (London: Methuen, 1982), pp. 145–46.

    13. Claude Lévi-Strauss, "Myth and Music," in his *Myth and Meaning* (London: Routledge and Kegan Paul, 1978), pp. 44–54.

    14. Eric D. Hirsch, *Validity in Interpretation* (New Haven, Conn.: Yale University Press, 1967), p. 25.

    15. Paul Ricoeur, "The Model of the Text: Meaningful Action Considered as a Text," *Social Research* 38 (1971), p. 547.

    16. Paul Ricoeur, *The Rule of Metaphor: Multidisciplinary Studies in the Creation of Meaning in Language* (London: Routledge and Kegan Paul, 1978), p. 23

    17. Ricoeur, "Model of the Text," p. 547.

    18. Ricoeur, "Model of the Text," p. 549.

    19. Ricoeur, "Model of the Text," pp. 542–43.

    20. Agee and Evans, *Let Us Now Praise Famous Men,* p. 111.

    21. Agee and Evans, p. 110.

    22. C. R. Moore, "Luke Lugomier," in Henry Reynolds, ed., *Race Relations in North Queensland* (Townsville: History Department of James Cook University, 1978), pp. 181–94.

    23. Moore, "Luke Lugomier," p. 193, n. 23.

    24. Agee and Evans, p. 319.

7. Yarning

In writing this chapter, I have relied considerably on the insights of Tom O'Regan, Brian Shoesmith, Stuart Cunningham, and Albert Moran. Their encouragement and enthusiasm have been crucial. Thanks to all.

1. Patrick Wright, *On Living in an Old Country: The National Past in Contemporary Britain* (London: Verso, 1985), pp. 61–62.

2. Margriet Bonnin, *A Study of Descriptive and Travel Writing, 1929–1945* (Ph.D. thesis, University of Queensland), 1980, p. 2; quoted in Meaghan Morris, "PANORAMA: The Live, the Dead and the Living," in Paul Foss, ed., *Island in the Stream: Myths of Place in Australian Culture* (Sydney: Pluto Press, 1988), p. 167.

3. Morris, "PANORAMA," p. 171.

4. Wright, *On Living in an Old Country*, p. 65.

5. Stuart Cunningham, "To Go Back and Beyond," *Continuum* 2, no. 1 (1990), p. 162.

6. Morris, p. 172.

7. William Lane, from *The Boomerang* (Nov. 19, 1887); quoted in Brian Kiernan, "Society and Nature in *Such Is Life*," *Australian Literary Studies* 2 (December 1963), p. 77.

8. Ivor Indyk, "Reading Men Like Signboards: The Egalitarian Semiotic of *Such Is Life*," *Australian Literary Studies* 12, no. 3 (May 1986), p. 305.

9. Miles Franklin and Kate Baker, *Joseph Furphy: The Legend of a Man and His Book* (Sydney: Angus and Robertson, 1944), p. 140.

10. Meaghan Morris, "Tooth and Claw: Tales of Survival and *Crocodile Dundee*," *Art & Text* 25 (June 1987), p. 50.

11. Cunningham, "To Go Back and Beyond," p. 162.

12. Cunningham, p. 163.

13. Cunningham, p. 160.

14. Cunningham, p. 162.

15. Charles Sturt, *Two Expeditions into the Interior of Southern Australia during the Years 1828, 1829, 1830 and 1831,* 2 vols. (London, Smith, Elder and Co., 1833); Charles Sturt, *Narrative of an Expedition into Central Australia,* 2 vols. (London: T. and W. Boone, 1849); Thomas Mitchell, *Three Expeditions into the Inte-*

rior of Eastern Australia, 2 vols. (London: T. and W. Boone, 1938); Thomas Mitchell, *Journal of an Expedition into the Interior of Tropical Australia* (London: Longmans, 1848); Edward Eyre, *Journals of Expeditions of Discovery into Central Australia,* 2 vols. (London: T. and W. Boone, 1845).

16. Tom O'Regan, in Ross Gibson, Tom O'Regan, Albert Moran, and Brian Shoesmith, "Interview: On *The Back of Beyond,*" *Continuum* 1, no. 1 (1987), p. 80.

17. Eric Michaels, *For a Cultural Future: Francis Jupurrurla Makes TV at Yuendumu* (Sydney: Artspace, 1987) pp. 30–31.

18. Cunningham, p. 160. Cunningham notes astutely how integral the role of women is in the film's portrayal of the Track's system of delegation.

8. Yondering

1. Mark Twain, *Following the Equator. A Journey Round the World* (New York: Harper, 1925), vol. 1, p. 150.

2. David Collins, *An Account of the English Colony in New South Wales* (London: Cadell & Davies, 1798), p. 6.

3. Germain Bazin, *The Baroque: Principles, Styles, Modes, Themes* (London: Thames and Hudson, 1968), p. 63.

4. Bazin, p. 44.

5. Bazin, p. 53.

6. Bazin, p. 10.

7. Judith Hook, *The Baroque Age in England* (London: Thames and Hudson, 1976), p. 11.

8. "Prologue" voice-over to *Mad Max 2.*

9. Remembering Art

1. Frances Yates, *The Art of Memory* (Harmondsworth: Penguin, 1969), pp. 18–19.

2. Quoted in Yates, p. 47.

3. For particularly useful examinations of eighteenth-century vision, see Marjorie Nicolson, *Newton Demands the Muse: Newton's "Opticks" and the Eighteenth Century Poets* (Princeton: Princeton University Press, 1946); and Maureen McNeil, "The Scientific Muse: The Poetry of Erasmus Darwin," in L. J. Jordanova, ed., *Languages of Nature: Critical Essays on Science and Literature* (London: Free Association Books, 1986).

4. See Jonathan Spence, *The Memory Palace of Matteo Ricci* (Harmondsworth: Penguin, 1985), p. 11.

5. Peter Brooks, *The Melodramatic Imagination: Balzac, Henry James, Melodrama, and the Mode of Excess* (New Haven: Yale University Press, 1976), p. 67.

11. Paranoid Critical Methods

1. Joyce Carol Oates, "Against Nature," *Antaeus* 57 (Autumn, 1986), p. 238.

2. Dana Polan, "The Critique of Cinematic Reason: Stephen Heath and the Theoretical Study of Film," *BOUNDARY2* 13, no. 2/3 (Winter/Spring 1985), p. 160.

3. John Docker, *In a Critical Condition: Reading Australian Literature* (Ringwood: Penguin, 1984); and Tim Rowse, *Australian Liberalism and National Character* (Melbourne: Kibble, 1978), respectively.

4. For a useful history of the idea of nature as the ultimate evaluative yardstick, see A. E. Pilkington's "'Nature' as Ethical Norm in the Enlightenment," in L. J. Jordanova, ed., *Languages of Nature: Critical Essays on Science and Literature* (London: Free Association Books, 1986), pp. 51–85.

5. See, respectively, *Electrical Storm*, Hot Records-Australia, HOTLP-1020; *A Portrait Chronicle, From the Book of Painting, From the Still Life, Work to Rule;* and *On the Beach 2* (1983), pp. 13–15.

Index

Index

Index

Index

ROSS GIBSON, Lecturer in
Screen Studies at the University
of Technology, Sydney, is also a
writer and filmmaker. His first
book, *The Diminishing Paradise:
Changing Literary Perceptions of
Australia* was published in 1984.
In 1991 he completed his first feature film, *Dead to the World*, which
he wrote and directed for Huzzah
Productions in Sydney.